Perfectly

Imperfectly

A

Mess

This book is a love letter to my trauma and strength. I dedicate it to my friends that have stood by me through all of the pain, sorrow and growth and encouraged me to always be my best self.

To my best friend Traci, my Jiminy Cricket, and my soulmate. God brought you into my life to not only guide me, but to show me what unconditional love and what true friendship is. You showed me that I am perfectly and wonderfully made in God's eyes and that bit of kindness and comfort changed how I looked at myself. Thank you is just simply not enough for you.

To all the many people that have persevered through any form of abuse and come out the other side. Maybe you are fractured, but you are not broken, I see you and I am with you.

Mrs. Robin Tassler at Miami Palmetto High School, thank you for believing in me and for always making sure that I was fed, felt loved and got to school. You changed my life more than you will ever know.

To EMDR and my therapist, Traci Withrow, without this therapy and your help, I would still be the cynical grouchy shell of a woman that I used to be.

To my two beautiful daughters who show me daily that not only am I enough, but I am loveable too; being your mom has been my greatest accomplishment, honor, and privilege.

Lastly, to God, for his unwavering love, faith, and constant belief in me and my flawed abilities.

This book is for all the perfectly imperfectly people out there that just happen to also be a mess.

Trigger Warnings & Resources:

This book is a memoir that depicts acts of sexual abuse, domestic violence, rape and mental abuse. It also discusses suicide. If that is triggering to you, please take this as a warning and choose to move forward free of your own will and choice.

National Center for Domestic Violence: *thehotline.org 1-800-799-7233*

RAINN: *@rainn (instagram)*

The Jamie Kimble Foundation for Courage: *@jkffcourage (instagram)*

Safe Alliance Charlotte: *@safe_ alliance (instagram) 980-771-4673 (24/7 hotline for sexual assault and domestic violence in Charlotte, NC)*

Peace Over Pieces Non Profit: *@peaceoverpieces (instagram)*

Suicide Prevention Resource Center: *sprc.org 1-800-273-8255*

Chapter One

And so it begins....

So, there I am, lying on the floor of my walk-in closet,

surrounded by empty chocolate wrappers and an empty wine bottle-ok, maybe two; sobbing uncontrollably, chocolate all over my face. I begin to wonder how I got to this point at almost 40 years old where I am a mess over a boy. How? My vision of what a loving man should be was influenced by movies and TV shows, not my father as it should be. Shit my ideal boyfriend was a cross between Kevin Costner in Robin Hood and Cary Elwes in The Princess Bride meets Maurice Bernard on General Hospital. You know the type. The guy who will protect you in such a graceful and intent way all while being super easy on the eyes. This same one is someone who you know you are completely safe with in every way, even your heart. Your feelings matter, your love matters...you matter. Someone a bit heavy on the playfulness, ya know, that special type of playfulness that calls you out on your shit daily and makes fun of you at the same time; lovingly though. Yep, super solid foundation here folks, he is attainable, I am sure of it. Some writers wrote him that way, so what if he is imaginary; he is possible. So what if he is an entire collection of bits and pieces of failed relationships and failed expectations? He is attainable; I am sure of it, or at least that is what these two bottles of wine and chocolate coma are telling me.

I realize in this chocolate and wine fog that I am not the best judge of love. I notice that I am still crying, this middle school ugly girl cry with a winestained smile and chocolate-covered teeth. We all know *that* cry, *that* feeling. It's the one where your parents tell you that you cannot go to the movies with a boy for the first time, or when they ground you and you are thoroughly appalled at them and life in general; ugh how dare they parent me. That was the cry. This odd mixture of an over-the-top Will Ferrell moment and total devastation, with a side of Saracco. That is me, dealing with the ending of a relationship I was positive that would never end. A relationship that I was convinced, I mean you couldn't tell me anything, would last. The relationship that I had been waiting my whole life for. This guy, Massimo, was perfect for me; in my head, at least. He was strong, charismatic, witty, called me out on my shit and I believed he loved me. He was my Italian Prince Charming. Who cares that he barely made a dollar in our relationship, who cares that I kept his lights twinkling, literally. Who cares that he teetered on the line of a full-blown manipulator and narcissist? He was perfect, to me; and he was mine. This fairytale of love and empty wallets seemed so amazing that I could never fathom an ending. But, an ending was what I got and now I sit here reminiscing, pondering, and questioning everything. In those moments of drunken vulnerability and hopelessness, I came to some pretty clear and definitive ideals. At the bottom of the bottle, I found clarity and began to wonder why I am great at friendships and terrible at relationships. I was, and am essentially, bad at love (cue Halsey music); like really bad at it.

It was perfectly clear to me. The true intimacy that comes in a relationship of love and romance was one that I was never able to learn appropriately, or never taught for better clarification. I was destined from conception to never truly get what true intimacy was, because of my childhood; but we will get into that! The intimacy I had with my friends was genuine, real, and unwavering. It was based on admiration, love, loyalty, honesty, and respect. The difference was there was no being intimate with my friends. With my friends, I could feel their love in how we spoke to each other and the fact that my real ones have seen me ugly cry without passing judgment! I have never questioned their love or my devotion to our relationship, but in romantic relationships, the questions are endless for me. My friends were those Hollywood men that I searched for, each one a little different, but all made perfectly for me.

Back to the ugly crying.

So, it was in this total devastation and sadness that I found some piece of solace and moments of clarity. A piece of me again, a missing piece. I began to write. I wrote everything, and I mean everything. I wrote about the delivery man that brought my Chinese food, and how comical I thought it was that he was a white man that smelled like cigarettes, always looked like he hadn't showered in months, and drove an Infiniti. I was intrigued at how this delivery guy had a better car than I did and how that place was ok with *him* as a representation of their restaurant. The grocery person delivering my food and wine (yes, there are delivery services for everything nowadays) always made me feel bougie and lazy when they came huffing and puffing up the stairs to haul my Moscato. It seemed like I was finding some sort of comfort in my thoughts, which was odd. I had always steered clear of them. Those little bastards have gotten me in a lot of trouble over the years and we had an understanding. You guys can come up with whatever cockamamy scenario you could, and I wouldn't act on them, but just be entertained by them. But now, I was strangely confident in them and it felt empowering and almost satisfying in some weird way.

I was beginning to have one of those feminist moments with my thoughts where I felt like I could walk around and be anything and do anything. I felt powerful and it was at that moment, I found kickboxing, Tony and a kickboxing gym that became a place that my frustrations went to die. My friend told me about it because he was a trainer there. I had seen his body transform from going there and I had seen his confidence soar; I had to check it out. I had always been fascinated with MMA and fighting in general so this wasn't a stretch for me to wanna fight. Shit, I still sit and watch YouTube videos of backyard brawls with fellow Panther Alum and Miami's own Kimbo Slice. I took pride in knowing that that brawler grew up where I did and went to the same high school as I did. I loved the idea of beating the crap out of someone. Of feeling so strong and confident that I could enter an octagon, ring, or wherever and square up with someone intent on hurting me and win. You will understand my need for channeling these thoughts later. When I walked in there for the first time to register, I felt at home, instantly. I felt that this was where I was supposed to be. Under the strobe lights and loud thumping music, I found what had been lost and I didn't know how to find it.

But, in further searching for my inner strength again, I found some comfort in kicking the shit out of bags and having my ass handed to me by these men that I paid to yell at me. More importantly, I found myself. But that came with a lot of exploration, ugly cries and acceptance, and bruises. It came with me saying, enough is enough. quit the bullshit, own up to your own shit, accept who you are and embrace it.

So, you are asking yourself, why should I care about this 40-year-old woman's life story?

You should care because my life story is probably more similar to yours than you think if you picked up this book. Or, maybe someone told you that you needed to read this book. Maybe you stumbled across it in Barnes and Noble (gosh I hope to make it there to the good table). Possibly, someone you love said, "Hey, here's this great book for you." Those are the best people in your life, by the way, the ones that think about you so often that they see things that remind them of you and get them for you to brighten your day or to enlighten your existence. They are the ones that know you better than you know yourself and think that this same book they are steering you towards will help you on your very own path to your self-discovery. My friend Alissa told me once that the best friends are the ones that you can share the books you've enjoyed with. Start handing this one out Alissa! I have the best friends!

If you have endured unimaginable pain, loss, fear, and unspeakable acts only to have come out of the horror, alive and stronger; this is my love letter to you. My story is mine and yours is yours. But, every single facet and nook are all that makes me who I am. Yours may be similar, or not even close, but you will never hear anything like it because it's mine to tell. I have found what was missing for me in this same story that I ran away from many decades ago, wore as a badge of courage at one time, and have been ashamed of all my life, and that was telling it.

My name is Kate, and I am not a survivor, I am a warrior, and this is my story.

Chapter Two

I was adopted shortly after birth. My birth mother and father were Puerto Rican, so I was told, come on Ancestry DNA kit results! I have minimal information about them, but what I do know is that they gave me to a family that they thought would be a better one than they could provide. You see when parents give their children up for adoption, it is the most genuine act of selflessness and love that can occur. You are unable to care for a child that you created and instead of trying, with the best of intentions, you give that child to a family that will do as you would or better; simply the definition of love; of pure selflessness. In my case, the beginning of my life was good. Years later, I was faced with this same choice and chose to raise my daughter. I can only imagine what my parents felt deciding to give their child up, and I may never know. I just know that I thank them for having the strength and courage to attempt to give me a better life. While a clumsy effort, it was an effort nonetheless.

I had a loving family and extended family. Two parents who were in love, two siblings who were also adopted, and a dog and cats. I mean this was some picture-perfect Leave It To Beaver shit. My mom was even a baking, sewing, stay-at-home PTO mom! I mean that shit doesn't even happen anymore. We had all the makings of a perfect adoptive family on the outside; crap they even featured us in The

Miami Herald a couple of times. My parents were these freaks of nature that fostered over 50 foster babies in their time fostering, another thing that doesn't happen anymore; and adopted just 4 of those. We always had babies and toddlers around from when my memories began. But, as all picturesque things look, there is always an imperfection, a blemish on the immaculate canvas. That thing that the artist hopes no one sees, but they only see when they look at it. You try to look at it from different angles, in different lighting, one eye covered, change your focus, anything to not see THAT flaw. But it always finds a way to show its inevitable ugly head. My family is like that scene at the party in Clueless where Cher and Tai are talking about Amber:

Tai: Do you think she's pretty?
Cher: No, she's a full-on Monet.
Tai: What's a Monet?
Cher: It's like a painting, see? From far away, it's OK, but up close, it's a big old mess.

My best friend of like a bazillion decades, Traci, brought this little gem to my attention. Traci, the woman that knows me better than I know myself and at times, I believe she is my very own Jiminy Cricket, my conscience. She told me that my family was that, on the surface type family. The one that everyone thought was Leave it to Beaveresque and we were more like Roseanne with a side of Precious, breaths away from a full-on CPS burst in or an episode of Law & Order SVU.

I don't think I can recall a time in my childhood where our home wasn't filled with children who were there briefly. My eldest brother,

Mark, was the first they adopted. The cutest blonde-haired, green-eyed child ever. The story is that he asked for a sister, and that he picked her out from the other babies at the orphanage. So there my parents were with 2 children, a boy and a green-eyed blonde-haired little girl with her own struggles, they could have been blood siblings they favored each other so much. My sister, Lizy, was born with cerebral palsy, a minor case, and her birth parents just couldn't tackle the lifelong battle that was to ensue. At some point in December of the late '70s, I was born. My parents and siblings had no clue what was about to be dropped on their doorstep. The lovely Catholic nuns brought me to my parents when I was 36 hours old, as a temporary foster. I was, as my father told me, a very sick baby. He has told me that he had to stay up with me night after night while I projectile vomited across the room and in those late vomit-filled nights, he fell in love with me. Ah, now I see why I can't find love, I am not vomiting on them; silly me.

Anyhow, a few weeks later the Nuns came to get me to take me to my next home, and my dad refused to give me up. He had bonded and wanted to keep me. It was in that act of love, that my whole life was forever changed. Who was that next family I was supposed to go to, how different would my life have been? I have never really dwelled on those questions because I believe that I was brought where I was supposed to be. So, there we were, all 5 of us and however many temporaries we had, living this happy life. And then, just like a tsunami, came my "brother" into our seemingly perfect lives and shit went to shit.

Interestingly enough, the few core memories I have are all with my older sister. Pick your mouth up Lizy, it's ok! I looked up to her, the way you are supposed to when you have a big sister. She was so cool to me and I wanted to be just like her. She always smiled and was nice to everyone. You see, I had a resting bitch face from birth, I noticed while looking at portraits done at Sears from my infant days. She lit up every room and I brought the gloom and doom. We were as opposite as they come and as we got older it became more prevalent. But, she was still my big sister and I was still her little sister. While being a rebellious big mouthed teenager, I got into some trouble with a girl who wanted to fight me. She came to my house after school and I was at work, my sister told her I was at work. She told me later that day that she felt like something was wrong, and she got in her car and came up to my work only to find I had just gotten into a pretty bad fight. I don't know if she came to check on me, watch, help, or what, but she was there when I needed her. She was my big sister at that moment and many others.

Now, my big brother, Mark, always knew I looked up to him. He was older, wiser, stronger, faster, and funnier; like all big brothers should be. He was protective, and kinda a jerk sometimes, but he wouldn't let anyone mess with me. When I was 17, he was the only person in my life I could be completely honest with. He married a longtime family friend that had always had a crush on him. Honestly, at first, I thought he married her just to marry someone or because of her connection to my mom. But as time has gone on, and I see photos and the life they have made, I don't think that anymore. She is warm, kind and funny. She is perfect for my big brother. As kids, I never was afraid if he was around. He had a larger-than-life personality at even a small age. We are not perfect, but he is my big brother and I love him.

Chapter Three

The "Brother"

He came to us from his, I don't know, maybe fifth

foster home and was already WAY fucked up when he got there. I was about three or four when he came. I don't have many memories from my childhood, after this, because I've blocked them out. So here comes the latest addition to our "happy home." Many of my friends after Middle School will not know him because he was gone before too long, but his presence and actions left life-long consequences and damage.

I don't remember the day he came, maybe I do and I just don't care to remember. Shortly after he had been around, after he was adopted and knew he wasn't going anywhere; my life changed. Before this, we were all happy, and laughing often. My mom was a huge practical joker and my dad was around, actually present. Things seemed as they should, happy. All the photos and memories from this time seemed pleasant and not gloomy. Again, I am not sure of the day or not sure if I am that everything changed. It happened almost instantly and all at once. There was no going back now, things were different. My world was different, my family was different; I was now different. I am sure that was the day my childhood left, that was the day that I grew up right there at 5 years old. That was the day that my happy childhood and photos of me smiling changed. The smiles became forced and the fear became real and lasting.

Webster defines the word "brother" as a man or boy in relation to other sons and daughters of his parents. By this definition, Scott was my brother. He was my parents' son and that in turn made him my "brother". By any other definition or meaning, that word should be identified that he was my destroyer; not my brother. Mark was my brother. Mark looked out for me, cared for me and protected me; as a brother should. Even as I sit here writing this, the ache in the pit of my stomach returns along with chills across my body and the hair on the back of my neck stands up. My voice trembles and my lip begins to quiver, I am shaking so much that the keyboard is unable to grasp what I am trying to say; so I switch to voice mode and even then it can't decipher the words through my trembling voice. It's amazing that so many decades later it still has the power over me to shake me to my core. There is no way to do this tactfully, so bear with me and take a deep breath with me while I blurt this out.

I don't remember again, the exact day it happened, but I remember EVERY single aspect of that night. My parents used to have a family movie night with us, or we would all lay in the living room on blankets beds we made on the floor watching TV as a family on the weekend evenings. As I write this, I can see that living room, that couch and my dad's old chair in the corner. My sister and I had this blanket from Disney World that meant the world to us. It had all the characters on it and a soft satin red border all around the whole thing. We fought over it constantly, and, at some point in our childhood, my father cut it in half and gave us each our own piece to stop the fighting. But, this particular night, it was still whole and I had possession of the treasure. I was lying watching some sort of family-friendly TV with my family and it happened.

My brother stuck his penis inside my vagina.

I remember laying there on my side in pain, silently crying, listening to him tell me in my ear that I can't tell anyone or they will send me back like him. I knew he had been in and out of foster care and foster homes, but this was the only home I knew. I also knew I was adopted, my parents were very open about that. I mean I was Puerto Rican in a home of Irish and Polish Americans, anyone could see I was different. I remember it was very brief, even though it seemed like it lasted for hours, but it did not. I remember lying there and feeling him on my back, he was so close to me and breathing so hard, his hot smelly breath on my neck telling me things that frightened me; while a tear rolled down my innocent cheek. I remember him finishing and I thought, "ok, this will never happen again and I have to be a good girl so they don't send me back." This was the night that I got skilled at sucking up my tears quickly and acting the part. My innocence left with every tear I couldn't let out, with every internal scream for help and the many sorrow-filled nights just wanting to tell. With every breath he forced on my neck, my childhood disappeared into thin air. I would never be the same. I would never be like my friends. I would never again be a child.

Many dreadful years continued like this and no one was the wiser. He would steal me whenever he could and sometimes when he knew he could get caught just to test it. I was his personal sex slave in a home that no one knew what was going on and I had to give my body to him when he wanted it and where he wanted it. Daily and sometimes multiple times a day this "brother" raped me in my picture perfect home. The place that my birth parents sent me to, where I was supposed to be safe and better off there than with them at their home. The same home that my father fell in love with me in, and decided to adopt me. The place I first crawled and walked and had birthday parties and baked with my mom. My safe haven had now become a dungeon of doom. A place that I never wanted to be or come home to.

The next 6 years were traumatic, to say the least. I did what I was supposed to do so I didn't have to be sent to another family. He told me I had to and I complied; I was always a rule follower and a good girl. I believe that this is where my need to please the man I am with comes from. He had convinced me over the years that my parents didn't want non-white kids and if they knew what he was doing to me that they would blame it on me and send me back to wherever I was afraid to go. I truly believed him and I truly believed that my parents could be swayed like that. I disconnected from everything in my life and everyone.

This "brother" shaped my childhood and destroyed it in one act of disgust. I have never felt whole and never felt the way some as my girlfriends have about sex and love-making. The act of sex or lovemaking was and has always been foreign to me because of my "brother", and he ruined it for me. He took away the beauty in the intimacy of making love and made it ugly, dirty and jaded. He justified what he had done to me by saying that because we were not blood it was ok. When he was sixteen and I was thirteen, my step mother told me that my parents were looking for some kind of boot camp place to send him because they couldn't deal with all he had been doing. You see, Scott was good at one thing in his life, baseball and he was bad at everything else. But, everything around him criminal, destructive and deceitful was more luring. Folks, this is proof that sometimes a child raised is a product of their environment and no matter what you do, they will be that.

He grew up in homes that were unsafe and criminal and was molested there in those multiple homes. So, no matter how much love, attention and good my parents showed him, his foundation was built before he walked through our door. Anyhow, my stepmother asked me if I knew anything about Scott that they didn't and advised me that this would be a good time to tell her. I remember her standing in the kitchen cooking, on a Sunday afternoon. She always cooked on Sundays for the week and sometimes, I could watch or help.

It was those moments with her that I felt the closest to her. It was in those moments, cooking, assisting, and laughing together that I was vulnerable and able to let her in; finally. Something came over me, and I thought that this was my chance; I could finally release this weight I had shouldered alone for so long, quietly. You see, my mom was sick and we lived with my dad and stepmother by this point. I thought that if my dad didn't want me anymore, I could go back to my mom, but I knew I had to finally tell. It was then that my voice shook and cracked and out it came. She had a hard time hearing and she asked me, "what did you just say?"

And I knew she heard me, but she wanted to hear it again, hoping what she had just heard through her hearing aid wasn't true. So, I told her again, this time the courage was coming through with tears and conviction in my words I spoke again confident and defiant in my declaration, "Scott has had sex with me from when I was 5 years old until I was 11 years old." She grabbed me instantly and every tear that I had sucked up for the last 6 years came out of me and I didn't suck them back up. I let them out. I finally breathed. I felt safe. I felt heard. She told me I had to tell my dad while wiping away my tears and hugging me in utter disbelief. I saw the change in how she looked at me in that hug. She never looked at me the same after that day.

We went into the garage where my dad was working out on the treadmill and she told him he needed to stop and he asked for a few more minutes and she demanded, "Honey, no, now" and he did; he always did what she said. He stopped his treadmill, turned around dripping in sweat, to see me crying and my step mother holding onto me and quite frankly, holding me up. I was so exhausted from carrying this lie through my life and now that I had released it, the only thing I wanted was sleep. He knew something was wrong, but not what was going to come out of my mouth.

Again, my conviction through tears came out with that phrase, "Scott has had sex with me from when I was 5 years old until I was 11 years old." When I told him, almost instantly, I watched as pity formed in his eyes and regret along with guilt. My dad grabbed me as if he was trying to protect me from when I was a child before Scott got to me. He apologized to me that I had this happen and cried right there in the garage, hugging me, she stood there watching. I don't think I had seen my father cry until that day. He was always this pillar of strength to me; tall, strong, masculine, intelligent, and funny. My dad could make me laugh harder than anyone and was always down to show me amazing music and sing in the car with me. When I was little, he always had me work on my mom's big van with him. We did oil changes and tire changes, he called me his Grease Monkey. Sometimes, I think there was nothing wrong with the car, that it was just the way he knew to bond with me and that was comfortable for him. Us covered in grease, drinking Tang and laughing while singing whatever song he played for me. My dad has a great voice. He used to sing me Brown Eyed Girl by Van Morrison all the time, I was his brown-eyed girl. I remember thinking it was so cool when I got to use the gooey stuff to get the grease off my hands and I got to dance and sing around the carport with my daddy. My dad and I ran together and laughed and played. He was my childhood hero. There was nothing he couldn't do in my eyes, except keep me safe. In that moment that I told him what Scott had done to me, I could see him looking for his little grease monkey; that same little vomiting child he fell in love with. It was like he understood why I had changed over the years, he got it; he finally got me. Definitely, in that moment being in my daddy's arms, crying uncontrollably, I knew this was the second time this man would rescue me.

Chapter Four

The Aftermath

$\mathcal{T}$he next days, weeks, months, and years for that matter

would be challenging to say the least. My parents did everything right,
then. They separated us, called the police, and got me examined and
in counseling and a youth group that the R.A.P.E. treatment center
recommended for other young sexual assault victims. Now, for anyone
that has been a victim of any sort of sexual crime, they know what this
exam is all about. It is by far the most degrading and violating exam I
have ever had and at points you feel as if your abuse has begun again,
it is that intrusive. I wish I could compare it to an AP English exam in
high school or a Biology final, but I would take those over and over
and for everyone in my class to never have to have done that exam and
felt so vulnerable and violated. I cried because it hurt and my
stepmother was with me the whole time. There was something in her
eyes that I had not seen before, except once.

Many months before this experience, we moved in with my dad and
stepmom full-time and away from my mom. To this day, I still don't
understand why or how that all transpired, and I think it is because
my dad wants to protect my mom's image in my mind; even though
it's tainted, again, explain later. Anyhow, it was Valentine's Day
morning and my mom left those CVS Valentine hearts with chocolate
in them, on the bumper of my stepmother's car. At this point in my

childhood, I was going through the, I hate my mother stage, and my stepmother was not having any part of it. She would encourage me to make amends with her and forgive her, but I am not sure I ever did. I took us moving in with my dad and her turning her back on us, even though we could still see her and talk to her, it was not the same; she wasn't there.

Anyway, when I went out to get the Valentine, I looked at it, almost disappointed in something. I remember that it had rained the night before and it was so sunny out now, but the chocolate hearts were covered in dew and they were ruined. My stepmother looked at me and put her arm around me and smiled and her eyes were filled with love, pity, and sadness for me. You see, my stepmother, that woman, and I have not always seen eye to eye on anything.

When I first met her I was young, around the same age as all of the Scott shit. My dad was a runner and so was she. They met during a race and they were both married. She had a son, James, that we would hang out with while my dad and she ran their race. Then we would all go our separate ways until the next race. I was always envious of how simply beautiful and elegant she was to me. She had gorgeous curly hair, and sophisticated class. You know that type of class, like the old Hollywood movie stars had, and along with that effortless beauty that they don't realize. That was Sandy. She was and is still the same. Always put together, lipstick in place, and a perfectly selected outfit she got on the Clearance rack at Marshall's. This woman was a woman I looked up to. She let me wear her long dangly earrings and I wanted to have my nails French manicured like her. She would play with my hair at the park after the races or before and I was always happy to see her. I still don't know how she went from running partner to life partner, but it happened at some point, while I idolized her. This woman shook up our family and the life we all knew. It was very easy to hate her, and not want to like her anymore, but if I am being true to myself, I always liked her and I always wanted to be like her. So much so that I pierced my ear because she had two holes in her ear and I wanted to have them the same. I chickened out and only got one ear done though.

My mom hated this woman, and I mean hated. I came home from a weekend with my dad and Sandy, and my mom full-on lost her shit on me. I had always admired Sandy's French manicured nails and asked her if I could have them, too. She asked my dad and he must have said ok because she painted my nails. I had never felt so close to her. My hand in hers and trying so hard not to move so I wouldn't mess up the lines. I was for sure gonna look as sophisticated as her, I was sure of it, I felt fancy! I felt beautiful and my dad made sure to tell me how lovely my nails looked. You couldn't tell me anything, I knew they looked flawless and I couldn't wait to show my mom how pretty they were. When I came home, my mom took one look at my nails and said, "only sluts get French manicures! Take that off!" I was devastated. What was a slut? Why was I one? Was this something that everyone knew about French manicured nails? I had to remove them and for a moment, my view of my stepmother changed, and she was now a slut trying to make me a slut too. Ah the sweet innocence of children. Obviously, a French manicure is not slutty and she was not a slut for having one, but you couldn't tell the 11-year-old inside of me that. It was clear my mom hated her, and like a loyal daughter, I too had to. To this day, I still get french manicured nails and feel that they are what make my nails prettiest.

Lying on this table having my vagina examined by a stranger, my stepmother holding my hand while I cried, this was a real moment of love. This woman never left my side. She never let me endure any of what was to come alone, unless the police asked to speak to me alone; she was by my side. She was my ride or die, for this brief moment in time. The exams were finished, the statements were given, the siblings were talked to and all that was left was Scott. He had to be talked to by the police at the station and because he was a minor, my dad had to be there so that they could talk to him. After my dad came home from the police station, minus Scott, I overheard him telling my step mother about it. He was upset, appalled and shocked. Scott told the police, "Yeah, I fucked my sister, so what?" So what? That is his admission? That is the release of guilt? Was there *any* guilt at all? I laid in my room that statement replaying in my mind and quietly sobbing; I was broken, overwhelmed, and they never knew I heard that.

After that dreadful exam, the rape treatment center referred me to group therapy for other girls my age that were raped. I remember being mortified that other girls had been through what I had been through. For some reason, I felt that it had only happened to me, ah that innocence again. I was so incredibly wrapped up in my own feelings about the situation that I couldn't fathom someone else's "brother" taking their innocence away like mine was. What I learned from the group and counseling in general was that no one was exempt from this heinous act of violence. Insert the Law and Order SVU dun, dun. No one was truly safe from it and it was not just brothers that did it. I was not the only one that was thrust into this in my own home, others were as well. And I found no comfort in this realization, just sorrow and self hatred.

I remember that this group met at a church, which I thought was quite cynical at the time. God is supposed to protect us from these abhorrent acts and yet here we were meeting to discuss and heal from them in God's house. Each week, we would bring a snack for the group, because we were all children and needed some sugary substance for the hour we sat in reflection and sadness. This one particular time, I hold it fondly in my heart. It was not too long after beginning with the group and my dad was still looking for his little grease monkey daily in me, we were driving to the group. I held my crumb cake Entenmann's donuts on my lap, so proud my dad let me get the good kind. My dad reached for my hand to hold while we drove. He hadn't done that in years. I think he sensed my trepidation and wanted to offer some comfort. Or maybe he needed some courage too. I could tell he wanted to ask me if I was still his little girl, or how I was doing and instead we talked about the weather and The Miami Hurricanes and skated around what we both wanted to say; I wish this never happened. Like clockwork, every Thursday my dad drove me to this group and waited for me. I sat in that church classroom and would listen to other girls tell their story and cry and be angry and then get stronger. I kept searching for my getting stronger moment, and it seemed so far out of my reach. I just continued going, mostly because my dad and I had our own time together again, uninterrupted and because he said it was what I needed; still never getting that "stronger" moment. When your hero tells you that you should do something you don't like, you follow blindly.

Chapter Five

The Parental Units

*N*ow, I am wondering a few things here. Is my dad

sitting in complete and total shock finding out that he was my hero and hearing my words? Is my step mother about to have a coronary at the nice things I have said about her? I am going to say yes to both! I was always a great writer, and great at expressing my feelings with words. In second grade, I won second place in a Father's Day writing contest about my dad. The Miami Herald published my words about my dad! It is (or so it was last time I was there) framed and hangs on a wall in my old bedroom at my parents house.

While no one could ever say that writing wasn't my niche, it was the other parts of relationships that I was awkward with. I am sure that there are at least 5 people that know me that are vigorously shaking their heads right now, including my ex-husband. I could highly respect you and yet still say "Fuck You!" ever so delicately. An unwelcome talent in my teen years, I perfected as I aged, and only gave up as maturity reared its ugly head; and consistent employment was vital. I find myself looking forward to a socially acceptable age where I can just walk around biting people and telling them to Fuck Off and not have to get into a fist fight. I am thinking that it is like 70, so come on 70!

Anyhow, back to my parental units' total shock and awe at my insights so far, well, strap in, it's gonna be a bumpy ride. My disdain for my parents, yes I said disdain, calm the fuck down! Comes from many years of conditional love, and conditional parenting. You see, my parents are fantastic at telling you what you need to do to be an acceptable child worthy of their love, admiration, gifts and praise. I think in my life, no I know, I have heard I am proud of you, once from my dad and never from my step mother. Now, you may ask why that is important? It is because we all as humans thrive on praise, recognition and acceptance, especially from those we love and admire; our parents specifically. We live to make those same people look at us in complete approval and strive to hear, "I'm proud of you." Right now, I can still smile thinking about my dad telling me he was proud of me, it was rare enough to revel in it. I only ever wanted to be accepted for who I was by my parents and still at almost forty years old am not. But, the real freedom came in me deciding not to care anymore and not to try to live up to their unrealistic expectations of what their child should become. I realized that while they may not ever be proud of me, I am proud of me and I like me. I gave up trying to be the perfect daughter and accepted my role as the family black sheep. Nice to meet ya. I am sure that they are hemming, and hawing and my sister and step brother are cursing me right now for hurting their beloved parents yet again. Well, tough shit! This is MY story, and I will tell it as I see fit whether you like it or not; your approval is no longer needed. Life is about challenges and life is not always pretty, but we choose how we live it. I choose to no longer be the black sheep of my family and to not care if that is how they see me.

To understand where this soap box moment came from, we have to go back to that car ride to group therapy with my dad, my crumb cake donuts on my lap and him holding my hand. The reason this moment is monumental for me and my childhood was that since my dad's affair with my step mother essentially ruined and blew up our seemingly Leave It To Beaver home life, my stepmother was his everything. We were no longer those important children that he carefully chose and loved. I was no longer that sickly baby he stayed up nights with and fell in love with. I felt like an obstacle, I felt like a nuisance. I never felt real love again in that house. I never felt understood or accepted in that house. That grand house in an area that was affluent and obscene. My dad had taken us from the poor side of town with his marriage with my mother to the big homes and better schools area of Palmetto Bay. We were no longer Ridge Rats, now we were full blown snooty patooties. I kid though, because I was never snooty and definitely not a patootie. But now we're surrounded by nice homes, and nicer cars and kids with better clothes than us. Talk about feeling out of place. My dad's Isuzu I-Mark looked like it belonged to the maid sitting in the driveway and it was only a matter of time before he upgraded. I remember going to that house after he purchased it. I was in awe. It had a huge front door and a swimming pool! We had big bedrooms and a big bathroom. I was amazed.

My step brother James got the biggest bedroom and biggest bathroom. We were told it was because he was going to live there full time and we were only there every other weekend. So we all had to share rooms. My sister and I are in one with my dad's sad bachelor pad twin beds and my brothers in the other room together. I remember thinking how unfair it was that there was another bedroom available and James got his own room. My siblings and I would discuss how James, AKA The Prince, could do no wrong and he was perfect and the rest of us were trash. My mom never missed an opportunity to agree with us and pretty soon after we were convinced, we now had to live there full time. So, does James give up his perfect room with a private bathroom? Nope. Do we all have to still share a room, yep and a bathroom; all while The Prince has his own domain. Total crap.

This, parents, is how you create resentment in your children and unnecessary jealousy. Naturally, we had chores and had to keep our rooms cleaned like most children do. That was fine, but I had so many more chores it seemed to me than everyone else. Probably because my mouth got me into trouble because they just kept piling up. Whatevs! Now, I did at the time, actually like my stepmother as a person. I could see that she made my dad happy and that made me happy. But I never wanted to give her the satisfaction of knowing I liked her. I write this carefully because I still don't want to give her that. I wanted her to work for it. I wanted her to show up for me daily if she wanted my love and respect, since she demanded mine. She told me once when I was being insufferable that, "You don't have to like me, you don't even have to love me, but you have to respect me." And she didn't play.

There were never food fights like my mom had done and we never played practical jokes on one another, it was a business like respect. The days of saying "pass the potatoes" and them actually being thrown to you were over. No more green linguine food fights from years prior. That business respect, I can only compare to that of what you have with your banker. Like I don't really like you personally Bob and word around town is you hit the bottle hard and often, but you make me a shit ton of money in my investments, so let's both rich white guy laugh and I will go about my day. It was that kind of respect I had for her. She never went to my softball games because James had soccer, and if she did go, I got a lecture about my effort on the way home. You see, my parents are highly athletic people. They are those "Fit Couples" you see in the gym that you silently judge and go home and eat a chocolate bar thinking about. Bitches. Those damn Fit Couples. My parents are like that. Insert hard eye roll.

They run marathons and have marathon gym sessions. Their whole lives center around eating right and exercising, while maintaining the ability to drink wine, because they cannot give that up! They always tried to encourage us to exercise and eat super healthy. So much so that when I was no longer living at that house, I began a long term relationship with Coke, Pepsi and sweet snacks. It was one of mutual respect and admiration, they spoke to me and I devoured them. This also began my unhealthy ways that my stepmother had NO problem pointing out. Growing up in that house, we never had sugary cereals or snacks and we only got sodas on the Jewish Holidays when family came over. Which I always found comical. We were allowed to have these unhealthy snacks on holy days, hmm. My parents took great pride in their healthy lifestyle and running seemed to make my dad a better parent.

When we were little, my dad would organize these races and we always got to go and help and it became like this running family we were a part of. My dad and stepmother met there, amongst the races and sweat they fell in love. I am still not sure how, but they managed to keep it highly secret for many years. Which is difficult when you run literally in the same circles. My mom must've known, she had to have. Every article you read in Cosmo about cheating, the women always say they knew deep down, so I have to believe that my mom knew. I think when people can be that deceitful for that long, it tells you something about their character. To be able to hold two different lives for many years is challenging, I would assume, but my dad did it. He never seemed bothered coming home to my mom, and sleeping in the same bed with her and doing his fatherly duties with us. He seemed content, I still don't know how he did it or how it happened. Honestly, I don't care.

My mom was more in love with the idea of being a mom and actually mothering us than being a wife, I think. Her children were her life and my dad eventually had to take a back seat to that and that is where I assume he began to look for a front seat in someone else's life. I can remember being young, maybe 7, and we were on our way home from my grandparents home in Hialeah. My parents began arguing in the car, now I don't remember my mom and dad ever arguing which is why this stands out to me. We got home and it continued. My mom threw an iron at my dad and I remember thinking what is going on here, we don't do this in this house.

I was always pretty loved by my mom, but the bond with my dad was different. I was his grease monkey and he was my hero. I would sit on the toilet in the mornings while he was shaving for work and he would put shaving cream on my nose. He would make me breakfast on the weekends and he attempted to teach me to ride a bike. I was never and am still not the most coordinated person, so bike riding was just not working for me. I am also as my father would say, "a big chicken." So naturally, anything that required me to be off the ground and mobile terrified me. He would try to teach me to ride and run behind me and as soon as he let go I would jump off like a spider monkey. It became exhausting for us both and he and I gave up.

I never really learned, because I didn't care to. I just wanted that time with my dad. It was difficult getting time with him when there were so many other forces pulling him away and a crap ton of siblings and foster babies. I remember going to work with my dad at his computer company and it was amazing, just me and him. There were these huge machines that I believe were actual computers, total 80's pre-MACbook life and we got to print things out on computer paper that back then had green and white lines on it. I would practice my writing in his office, because my mom insisted on perfect penmanship. I would make him drawings for his walls, the same walls that were particle board and dark. I would try to lighten them up with color. My dad would let me shift the gears in his car when he drove. He would yell out, "2nd, 3rd, reverse" and I got to do it, with his help of course, but still, it was our thing. It was awesome! I couldn't understand when my dad left, why he left, we had created so many wonderful memories, why did he have to leave now?

My dad got this two story bachelor pad in Miami Springs near my Aunt and Uncle on my mom's side and we would go there one night a week and every other weekend. It was different. The place was never home and when we weren't there, we could tell that he wasn't either. I remember one time we were there, my dad was cooking dinner and Lizy and Mark were watching TV; Scott made me go upstairs. He held me down and raped me on my dad's bed with his hand over my mouth and my daddy just cooking dinner down stairs oblivious. He yelled up to us that dinner was done and I came down a few minutes after Scott because what he had just done hurt worse than other times. This one was rough and painful like I was being punished for something. I remember lying there hoping and praying that someone would come upstairs looking for us. I tried to call for my dad, that was why he covered my mouth and then he got forceful. This was one of the last times he raped me. There were a couple others that were not as aggressive, but rape nonetheless.

Anyhow, daddy wasn't there long, he eventually moved into Sandy's. At the time she was still Sandy, and she had a townhouse in another area of town not far from dad. It was not big enough for us all and we were cramped on our weekends. My sister and I slept on what used to be a patio that they enclosed for another bedroom. It had a door that led into the master bedroom and we had to go through that room to get out of the room. One of the first nights we slept there, I woke up in the morning, nervous to walk out of the room and hungry. I opened that door and saw what traumatized me for a few years, my dad and Sandy were making love. It was weird and awkward and gross. No one, I mean no one should ever see that. It was like the sheets and them having sex was burned in my retinas. Years later I would always have some trepidation laying in my parental unit's bed knowing they did stuff in it. Weird, I know, but I am weird.

In an effort to please my exercise loving parental units, I began running in track meets at Tropical Park in my teens. I literally sucked at this. I was short and stumpy and not made for high jumps, long jumps and shot put. I was however semi fast and did well in sprinting. My dad took pride in watching us out there. He finally had a child interested in what he was interested in. You see my dad loved running, I mean in every way. He would watch the New York City Marathon on TV every year and he ran in countless marathons across the country in my lifetime. He always found a new way to challenge himself and never gave up. So, with 4 children and a step child all doing different activities, to have one interested in his interest was important to him.

Mark was interested in band and music, Scott was only interested in baseball, Lizy was interested in cheerleading and gymnastics and James was interested in soccer. I played softball, and I did cheerleading and minimal gymnastics, to which I was awful at. I was never as graceful as my sister in her rhythmic gymnastics class. I was more of a giant screaming Fee Fi Fo Fum, while she was a fairy floating around. My sister was also extremely flexible and I could barely maintain a split. The boys all played baseball, but Scott stayed with it and was good at it. Mark is a phenomenal musician. He plays a gorgeous bass and that was what lit his soul on fire, that and surfing; as kids it was skateboarding.

So, I became interested in track and Lizy came along too and then the boys. We all did it, as a family. Lizy was good at the long jump. She was like this long legged frog that could leap across the sand in the swiftest way. Scott was super fast, like the flash, he was very good at all of the running stuff. Mark, prefered to be in the stands. I think my dad actually organized these events, but I still chose to believe he was there because he was happy we shared his interest. My dad encouraged you in this way that you didn't realize he just did.

It was slick and parental and warm all at the same time. My mom would come and hide up in the stands and when I would see her we would meet in secret for a quick hug. She hated my stepmother, she called her the wicked witch, so she never wanted to be seen anywhere that she was. Which is why I think that my stepmother never made it to many of our games. Baseball and softball was my moms turf, and she must've made that clear.

My mom had a special bond with the coaches that Scott played with and the families since the boys had played for many years together. That is actually where I met my first love, and best friend, Shawn. We were little kids watching our older brothers play baseball and we hung out in the dirt. He would later in life become the most treasured male relationship in my life, but at 5 years old he was just my friend Shawn with the long blonde tail. The brothers all played football and baseball together, so we saw each other year round and since Shawn and I were the same age, I was a cheerleader for his football team. My mom and other parents and coaches were quite friendly. This was a time when coaches from one sport took interest in a kid and watched them play anything that they played. This one tan skinned blue eyed coach was my favorite, Ron. He understood the game of baseball the way very few people did. He didn't have any children, but he was always at the fields. He coached and would watch games scouting the kids he would want on his next team. I think my mom had a crush on this car salesman with the pretty eyes.

After she got comfortable being divorced, she started going to every Miami Hurricanes Baseball home game with him and we would get to go too. We never sat in an actual seat. This guy preferred to watch the game behind home plate, he said that was the best seat in the house; which sucked for me cause I am super short. Watching those games behind home plate made me want to be a catcher. I watched Charles Johnson play game after game and I would try and emulate him standing behind him. He was this giant force that commanded plate respect and could throw you out from his knees without even removing his mask. It was this one swift majestic motion that he changed my view of the position and made me want it. Ron gave me a new appreciation and love of the game watching it with him. So these relationships we all built, my mom built, are the reasons why I think my stepmother backed off and didn't come. And if she did, I never can remember.

Chapter Six

Thirteen to Fifteen, the difficult years

$\mathcal{T}$hirteen was a particularly difficult year for me. My

hidden secret had been exposed and my mom had a massive heart attack. I remember going to visit her in the ICU and this woman that had always seemed indestructible to me was fragile, but she still made me laugh. She was not weak in mind, just body at the time. My grandmother blamed my dad for her heart attack even though it had been years since the split and divorce, it seemed an appropriate use of blame to her. My dad had been in the Air Force with this family friend, Dr. Dicky, and he and my mom remained in touch.

Somehow, he worked some kind of magic and my mom was given a new heart. Now, this could all be bullshit. You see, my mom had a big flare for the theatrics of a story. We all know those type of people, the ones that can turn a simple incident into an hours long play starring themselves. This was my mom, she was the epitome of funny with a side of the theatrical and it is what made her great. Anyhow, so, Dr. Dicky swooping in and saving her heart may actually be total shit, but nevertheless that is what she said. I think that she also needed to embellish all he did for her because she needed to feel like he was her Prince Charming since my dad was now her Sheriff of Nottingham. She was still wounded from what my dad had done to her and Dicky came in when she needed an ego boost and reminder that she was still a woman and could still be desired. She was in love with Dr. Dicky but he was in love with California and his life there, I believe she would have moved there if he asked her to. I know that they had a brief romance and he gave my mom her confidence back and that was pretty important for her.

So, armed with a new heart and new found confidence, my mom met Howard. The man that arguably should have been my step father. He was a bachelor with a huge Marmaduke great dane, and I was naturally a chicken around it. He seemed to love my mom and us kids and accept us. They seemed happy together in his home in the Gables. But, I think he couldn't commit to her the way she wanted. My mom got sicker over the years and we saw her less and less. I am not sure if it was that we didn't want to go or if she was not well enough to see us, but Mark was with her. Mark moved in and out of dads faster than I had a period. He couldn't stand Sandy, none of us really could if we are all being honest, Lizy included, and he couldn't stand my dad at that time. He felt loyalty to mom and that was where he was going to be. He worked many jobs to help mom out and help his band out.

One Saturday night, I got a call from Mark on my sister and I's private line. We had this neon see through phone on it and an answering machine, we thought we were hot shit! Anyhow, I was 15 when that call came through, and it was that call that would change my life. He was telling me that mom is really sick and in the hospital and she wanted to see me. My first thought was, she wants to see me and I have been a wretched and awful teenager staying away trying to adapt to my new life and just completely being angry with her. You see, my mom didn't believe that Scott had raped me. She didn't believe that those things occurred under her roof. The same roof that my dad cheated on her under, the denial was strong. So, in her not believing me, I wrote her off and stopped taking her calls and visits. I felt hurt, unacknowledged and betrayed as a teenager; so, you hold onto those assumptions and accusations and wear it like a fur coat in the summer.

So, of all people, I couldn't understand why she wanted to see me. I was awful to her and said some incredibly painful and shitty things out of anger and disapproval of her disbelief; and with a bit of encouragement from my step-monster. But, I assumed that this was what they meant when they said a mother's love is unconditional, so I waited for my brother's friend Henry to show up and pick me up. Mark, Henry and I made the trip to Jackson Memorial where my mom was in the Cardiac ICU; it was about a 30 minute drive in Henry's van that smelled like boys and food. Mark led the way, and I remember thinking what a great friend Henry was to my brother to take me up there and be there for him while all this was going on with mom. We make it on the CICU floor and it is dimly lit and serene with the sounds of machines echoing in a symphonic beat. The floor was surrounded by glass sliding doors with curtains in front of them and lights down low or completely off in each room. The nurses station was filled with warmth and smiling nurses that didn't bear pity on their face, just love and care. I strangely felt safe and whatever was behind one of these glass doors was going to be ok.

I walked behind Mark and Henry almost in slow motion, taking in all that was around me, all while not wanting to see my mom in pain again. Not wanting to see whatever was behind her sliding glass door. Would she be fraile again or would she be cracking jokes and reassuring me that she is ok? What is she doing here and why didn't I know sooner? Why would she be here and not tell me? Gosh I don't want to go in. Going in means that whatever is behind that curtain is real and I have to face it. I am not ready. Please don't make me. Mark turns back to smile and grabs my hand, tenderly and in the most protective big brother way. I think he knew I was freaking out inside and unable to process what had been his life for however long she was in there. He was stronger than I was. He was experienced and seasoned in this hospital floor and its ways. I was like a baby deer standing for the first time, stumbling through this floor until we got to her room.

We get to these sliding glass doors in this dark room lit only by the outside sunshine, and there is a faint green curtain and Mark slides the door open, surely my mom is not in there! We walked in quietly and there were machines everywhere, beeping in unison, almost melodic and tranquil. It seemed like every machine that was available in the hospital was in that ICU Suite and they were all working together to keep her alive. She looked up at me and I saw, my mommy, she looked frail, tired, and scared. I couldn't believe that this was the same woman that used to play practical jokes on us every April Fools, and the same woman that made our birthday cakes from scratch. My mom was *that* mom, the one that was fun and exciting all the time. She instigated food fights at the dinner table, pushed mashed potatoes through her front teeth and came up with the most elaborate April Fools jokes on us that she had us believing in year after year. So seeing her like this, with an oxygen mask on her face, in this state was traumatic, to say the least. It is like when your idol turns out to be not so blemish free and you feel empty. That was how I felt standing in that doorway, all the hate I had carried washed over me and left the moment I crossed the doorway. Why was she so frail and sick? Why had I been such a wretched teenager? All I wanted to do was forgive her and turn back time.

My mom lifted her breathing mask, said "come here beaner, it's ok" and reached out her hand for me. I looked back for reassurance from Mark that it was ok and he said it was, so I moved forward to her, leaving all the anger and hate behind. Those few steps seemed like hours and yet I found myself gliding to her and wanting to lay in the bed with her and hear her tell me it would all be ok. Henry waited in the background, quietly, patiently, protectively. I grabbed her hand and it felt the same; warm, and like home. She tried to crack a joke and we all chuckled, and she asked Mark for some privacy after a few moments. She asked me where my sister was, and Lizy didn't want to come, but I didn't tell mom that. She stared at me for a few moments, studying my face and holding it in her hand. She turned her smile so bright and happy and fought the mask for an unobstructed view of me. It was magical and momentous and the epitome of a mothers love. She was afraid and I could see it in her eyes, that, and the pain she was in. I wanted to stay there forever and be by her side; God had different ideals. We laughed and talked and mom laid there telling me many life lessons, anecdotes and advice all while struggling behind the mask. She wondered about my life now and then she started asking about Shawn. I told her that he finally kissed me and he was my first kiss and it was just as magical as every story book first kiss and Disney movie. I gushed about him and how happy he made me, but I told her he had moved away to Daytona Beach and we would probably have to break up. She said, "You're going to marry that Shawn Bartlett some day" I laughed, and knew it to not be true, but she seemed to need it. She asked me about my friends, and my life and genuinely cared. I think that she wanted to know that I had a support system behind me should I need them.

I told her about reconnecting with Traci and she remembered her and her mom fondly. We talked about cheerleading and softball and the Miami Hurricanes and we planned that she would take me to games when she was out of the hospital and better; she loved talking with me, she loved me for me, no conditions. I had been so angry with her for not believing me that I wasted two years. Everything she wanted me to know or hear, she said and answered. She told me that day that she knew that Scott had molested me. She knew and didn't know how to stop it. She begged me to forgive her and I gave her what it seemed that she needed. She looked like she was going to die, she assured me she wouldn't, and I told her I would have Henry bring me back on Friday after summer school to visit again. All week I thought about what would happen if she died. How would it be? How would I be? Would she be at peace? Was my forgiveness enough for her to peacefully be? My week continued and I went to summer school. It was my first year in High School and I was so nervous. That was the same summer that the love of my life to date moved away, Shawn Bartlett. Sophomore year, new school, just nerves and anticipation followed by high school football boys! I took typing and Drivers Ed that summer. I planned to try out for the school softball team, and I was going to make High School my bitch. I had my best friend Traci, and some other kick ass friends and we were all going to rock 10th grade. Friday morning, I woke up early, the bus came at 6:30 and we had to be ready to go a few minutes before. Something felt off to me, I felt sick to my stomach and I had a pain in my stomach. I started to cry, but I couldn't figure out why. The pain was not nearly tear-worthy, but tears flowed nonetheless. My dad came into my room and asked me what was wrong, I said, "I don't know." I just remember looking at the clock and it was 6:06am and I felt empty. I went to school and about my day. When I came home, I came through the patio by the pool to walk to my parents room. My step-mother was always waiting on her bed with her french doors open waiting for us to come home from school. She told me to go put my things down and come back. She had to talk to me. That whole walk to my room and back to hers was like the Green Mile, I had no clue what they had caught me doing, but I was just sure I was in trouble. Every possible thing I had done, I played through my head. I was always in trouble, so this walk was familiar, almost comfortable and I did it with swag in my step and a smirk on my face, and took solace in taking my time to come back to her room. Why rush if I was going to just be yelled at and grounded?

We started some small talk about school. I kept thinking, "spit it out, what did I do this time". She was dragging out whatever she had to say, and then she turned towards me and grabbed my hand in hers and leaned in close to me. She said to me, "I don't know how to tell you this, but your mom passed away this morning." I remember sitting there and not really grasping what she said. I remember asking if I could still go to my friend's house for my sleepover. I remember asking if my sister knew. Much more than that, I remember thinking how I should react. How do I not hurt Sandy? Now we were getting along swimmingly, and how can I not feel empty when my mom is gone. I asked one question, "what time did she die?" Sandy replied, "6:06am this morning." Now, my tears, that deep ache in my stomach all made sense. I asked if I could still go to my friend's house for the sleepover that was already planned and she agreed.

Going to my friend's house that night was a huge piece of controversy and speculation many years later and something that Sandy would throw in my face often as her "proof" that I didn't care that my mom passed away. Um, I was 15! Grief is different for everyone, there is no play book or list to check off and follow on how to grieve, I am sure people would like it though. It sure would make grieving a lot easier if there was a checklist. Cried today, check. Smelled your clothes, check. But, leaving that house that night to go to a friend that I felt safe with was what I needed. We stayed up all night, her and I talking with her mom and crying, laughing and eating brownies. What Sandy never knew was, I never felt that I could mourn my mother in front of her. I never felt that I could truly feel the gravity of this incredible and immeasurable loss in front of a woman that my sister was now calling mom knowing all too well that she despised my mom. I tried to conform like Lizy did and call her mom, but it never tasted right, it still doesn't. She questioned me in such a way that I knew I would never respect this woman the way she is begging me to. It was what I needed to process my mom's passing along with my guilt for how I had treated her for the past couple years, and I knew I would not get that with Sandy and Dad at my home. The adult me now knows that me needing to go to a friend that night was normal and what a child does to process death. Children strive and search for normalcy and structure in a time of loss, according to my EMDR therapist. So, for many many years, this woman made me feel like such a shitty person for doing something she deemed as insensitive and uncaring when in fact it was completely normal. Way to parent, bitch, and you wonder why I despise you, hmm!

That morning's tears made sense. That pit in my stomach made sense. But nothing else made sense, everything was just awful and different now. To this day, my stepmother questions the validity of my feelings since I wanted to go to that sleepover. So, my new mission with her then was distance and resistance. Keep her close enough to make her think you respect her and then pull the wool over her eyes. It was calculated, painful, deceitful, exhausting and mean, but so was she. To defeat the deceitful, you must become just like them, and I embraced that like a turtle neck. This woman that my father loves, my sister calls mom and my brother, my once loyal brother now has a relationship with, to me is satan. She is the puppet master and she pulls everyone's strings all while having on her perfectly planned outfit and manicured nails and hair. Not a single thought or move is made in my family without her approval. I never needed her validation after that moment and thus I was disposable and an orphan. She's like the Jewish Don of the family. Powerful beyond words, and trivial on the surface. But that calculated mind is something to be studied and frowned upon. She is wretched. She really is that wicked witch my mom always called her.

Chapter Seven

I am loveable!

*Y*ou're probably starting to see that I dislike my stepmother and are wondering why? Well, as a scorpion will always be a scorpion, people always show their true selves. She and I share some similarities, which is why I think I can see her for who she is and others simply cannot. She fools others with her thoughtful, calculated sweet gestures and smile, but never me; I saw through her the moment I truly met her. She can be infectious and warm and that is how she lures you in. Those that know me and know her get it and my therapist pegged her by session two. They get that she is a manipulative woman that will do what she can to get her way in whatever way she deems fit in her twisted mind. She has had a lifelong "illness" since I met her and it seems that some days she is "worse" than others. That is what she uses to pull you in, her sickness, her inability to function on a daily basis without her dramatic sickness.

She gets close, and then you start to let her in and confide in her; which she holds in her vault to use against you later. Then she learns everything that you will let her learn about you; your likes and dislikes and writes them down so she doesn't forget. It allows you to feel special when she remembers something you told her long ago. You start to get little cards in the mail, and trinkets, and think how sweet she is; she remembered you. Before you know it, you find yourself thinking, "Sandy is vital to my life", that's when she has won and you are in trouble. Without you realizing it, now she has you. Like a black widow spider in her net, you are stuck, you can't break free and she begins to devour your soul and your identity piece by piece until she has removed all she doesn't like, and you are a carcass. Then she starts to rebuild you the way she thinks that you should have been and she belittles you and attacks your insecurities along the way. Before you know it, who you once were is gone, and you are left with a carbon copy of her or who she wanted you to be. Almost a Stepford wife, just like she strived to become.

I was never the daughter she wanted. I was never the daughter she signed on for. My sister, she was. She was formed into her ideal child, the one that she had wanted. She was polite and at times poised and respectful and did as she was told. I was brash, aggressive and never did as I was told; more bull in a china shop than dainty princess. I questioned everything, always, and I still do. She couldn't mold me into what she wanted, so she befriended a friend of mine to do that. She has latched onto her so tight and attempts to make me jealous of their relationship at every step. I don't feel jealousy when I see the images of them together, I feel pity. I feel pity for her that she had to go find a replacement me, or a 2.0 version of me, because she really wanted the original but couldn't handle her. I feel pity that she has to try and manipulate others to make herself seem superior. My best friend once told me that her mother thought my stepmother was Bat Shit Crazy, that was the validation I needed. Traci's mom is much like my mom. The after school baking, caring, loving mom. The mom you respect and admire. So that she felt how I felt about Sandy was validation enough for me. I had always thought it was just me. That I was unlovable, that I was not worthy of her love, but it was her. She was the insane one, while she tried to pawn that off on me.

Now, my feelings aside, she makes my father blissfully happy and he is oblivious to her manipulations and destruction of others. It took me many decades and a lot of swallowing my pride to admit to that. She is whom my father should have been with all along. She is his person, his other half and his soul mate. They fit together and she is who he needs to be happy. Not me, not my sister or brothers, her. Without her, he would not survive and he has told me a few times that she is the only person he needs in his life, not any of his children. Those same children that my mother and him carefully selected and loved, he never wanted. When you hear your father say he never wanted you, something inside separates, and you can't quite figure out what way is up or down.

My stepmother is my dad's motherboard. I use a computer term, because my dad is a computer nerd. So, without a motherboard, your computer is just a box with no real function. She is his motherboard. She is his function. She is his purpose. She is who his heart beats for, not his children or grandchildren. He has told me in the past that she meant more than any of us to him, she knows this fact as well and has no problem throwing it in your face for reaction or spite.

It was around the same time he voiced a single sentence that would ring in my ears until the day I die. A sentence so overwhelming, so defeating, so damaging that it's full intent is to cause hurt and confusion. My "father" told me, "you are just unlovable". He carried on with the rest of whatever belittling things he had to say, but the damage had been done. I heard nothing further. I was empty. He finally said the one thing that would push me away for the rest of my life, and his. He finally crossed the line. This same man, that had always been my hero, that had always been a pillar to me; now just destroyed me and everything I thought I was. It was in that same conversation, which was followed up by a letter that he needed to finish his thoughts on, that he forever changed our relationship and it's meaning to us both.

This letter again, housed some insightful and damaging words again just used to cause pain and inflict hatred. "You are no longer my daughter. You are an orphan." Yep, my own dad, the one that chose me and nursed me to health and let me be molested for years while he was off fucking that bitch and playing daddy to her son, told me he never wanted any of us, my mom wanted kids and he went along with it! Now, I am sure you wondered why I used the word disdain before to describe those parental units of mine, I bet now you are beginning to understand my use of disdain and my merited anger towards these people. This man that swore and promised to love me, nursed me to health, gave me his last name has now thrown me aside for a piece of ass! I was not wanted, welcomed or loved any longer and they both made sure I knew just that. A child is not something that you throw away when they don't abide by your ideals and rules, you nurture them more, not abuse them emotionally, verbally and mentally.

My "parents" were one million percent verbally, and mentally abused me. Now, I played my own part in the words and actions that they chose to use, but I am not responsible for how they treated me and what was said to me and about me. In their story, I will always be the ungrateful, villaines daughter that is an utter disappointment. In mine, they will always be the people that I ran away from at 17 and didn't try to get me to come back; and I never looked back. I ran barefoot that day in a glorious moment of freedom and didn't care that I left behind them and all of my possessions. They will always be the people that told me I was an orphan and unlovable. They will always be less than, to me. I deserved parents that would never give up on me and parents that loved me unconditionally and supported me. I didn't get that in them. That was what my birth parents gave me up for. So I could be loved like they would and have parents that supported and adored me. I didn't get that from my mom either for that matter. I was essentially on my own since my mom gave me up. I fought for myself and was now, once again, an orphan.

Now if I know anything, I know he has never known how damaging that sentence was to me until now. I never gave him that satisfaction and struggled with giving it to him now, he doesn't deserve it. Shit, he had picked me after all to love and now he picked me to hate. I wore that like a goddamn tiara and dared anyone to try and touch it. I polished it and made its unloveable sparkle shine. You could not tell me I deserved to be loved. You could not tell me that you loved me and expect me to believe it. It took many years, and one insightful sentence from a person that will be my person forever. Traci told me, "I chose you as my friend every day and God chose you for my friend. He made you perfectly in his eyes and that means you are lovable."

Say WHAT! How lucky am I! This amazing woman with a god fearing heart chose me to be her best friend and loves me just the way I am; flaws and all! My own father can't love me that completely and unconditionally. Those words she told me have always rang in my heart like a tune that no one can hear but us. I never wonder if I am loved, I never question it anymore. My *best friend* loved me better than my parents ever could. I don't need to hear my father's description of me and my worthiness, I had Traci and God in my corner. God made me perfectly in his eyes, however flawed I am is just what he chose for me. But you know what, he also gave me a heart large enough to never stop loving my father; despite all that has been said and done. My heart is forgiving, strong and life changing. It is the heart that God made for me and it has sustained many breaks and fractures, but it still beats to the beat of it's own drum; your approval is not needed bandaids and all.

Chapter Eight

The Penguins

*A*s a mere toddler, I was enrolled in a Methodist church

day program called Crum Kids. It was there that I learned to color, run and play and potty. It was also more importantly, where I met my lifelong friend, my soulmate, Traci. Our moms would drop us off there for a mother's morning out type program where we got to play and socialize with other kids. Mostly, the mom's got a break from parenting for a few hours a day. The photos from that time show us with bad 80's haircuts and clothes and they are quite comical. Now, as toddlers, I can only imagine that we were thick as thieves, but we parted for our Elementary years and reconnected in Middle School. That summer before 7th Grade, my siblings and I moved in with my dad. I was going to have to go to a new Middle School. That was the summer of Hurricane Andrew. We were on vacation at Captiva Island, one of my favorite spots, and we awoke to find that we had hours before the storm would wreak havoc on our area. I was so mad we had to leave, because Captiva was where I always felt the most happy. There amongst the white sandy beaches and cats paw shells, I felt content. I loved to walk the beach and pick up shells. My mom used to have a lamp that was filled with all the shells we had picked up over the years. Cat paws were my favorite and I always searched for one that was fully intact, since most were chipped or completely broken.

School was supposed to start the next day, and it looked inevitable that we would get hit from this storm and school would be delayed. So, my family went into survival mode. My dad and brother put up shutters, my sister and I cleaned tubs and my step mother tried to grab whatever groceries at Publix that she could for us. Our house boarded up, we sat down to eat dinner as a family and watched the local weather report. The winds were starting and Sandy kept running to the kitchen window to assess the outside damage; it was the only one without a shutter. I remember my step mother crying while she watched our screened in patio drop into the pool. I thought then that she was being awfully dramatic, but now, as an adult, I realize it was watching all my dad's hard work blow away that was overwhelming to her. At some point we all ended up in my sister and I's bathroom because it was the largest and we could all be together. My dad stood guard at the pool patio door, while my step mother guarded the door into the bathroom. The sounds were overwhelming, scary and consistent. My sister tried to distract me and then she couldn't anymore and then my step brother tried, but we were all just too scared.

The wind blew out my bedroom window and then door, right across the hall from the bathroom and my step mother was unable to stop the sound of the door flying back and forth. It was bothersome to her because of her Meniere's Disease and she was trying to be strong for us so we weren't scared, but I am sure she was thinking we should've stayed in Captiva. The pressure in the air caused my brother's toilet to explode. That sound was as you could imagine. It was like a bomb went off on the opposite wall and I just remember being afraid we were going to die and wishing my dad had made us stay in Captiva at

Tween Waters Inn, where we were safe instead of going home. The storm passed after sounds that will haunt anyone from that area's thoughts.

As I write this, chills are all over my body because it was THAT traumatizing. Anyone that lived through that storm can tell you very detailed information and it will almost always include the use of the sounds. The winds made this music that resonated and suctioned itself to you and your memory. This terrifying cross between aggressive rain, howling winds and train whistle sounds as the tornado touched down and went down my street. I had not seen my dad cry often, but he cried. That was a sound I never was comfortable with. My dad was never a super emotional man, and I can't remember ever seeing him cry and this was the year I saw it twice. This was a defining year. The storm destroyed many homes and hopes in the surrounding areas of Miami-Dade County and friends lost more than anyone imagined. My new Middle School at the end of the block lost portables and the desks were in our front yard and through our trees.

The National Guard showed up a few days later, and my dad and brother could stop guarding us at night now. I can remember the sounds of looters in our backyard and my dad yelling for them to go. It was a scary time. It was so hot that August and the cleanup from the storm gave no one any relief from the heat. It was a constant stagnant heat that was a definitive reminder of what we all had just endured, mixed with the wretched smell of dead fish from the lakes that had overflown. We now went to sleep listening to The National Guard walking our streets and driving in their humvees. The schools opened back up a few weeks later and that first day, I walked up to school and saw Traci. See, Traci and I had met in Summer Camp at Coral Reef Park and sort of hung out, but we were not really "friends" yet. She was standing there talking to Andrea and Mindy and I thought these white girls are very different from Mays Middle School, the mostly hispanic and black school I had just left.

It took a few weeks, but Traci became my friend. We started hanging out on the weekends. She lived just under a mile from me and I would walk over to her house on Saturdays and we would walk up to the park and hang out. Most of the time I was supposed to be mowing lawns or washing cars and my parents wouldn't let me come back home until I had done one or the other. So I would leave early in the day, walk to Traci's and then hang out with her all day and on the way back home, I would stop at the same house every week and wash their car for $20. I did what I was supposed to do and never got caught and I got to hang out with Traci every weekend. It became a running joke that I had to leave so I could make some money before returning home. One of our times hanging out, Traci's mom had found some preschool pictures of Traci and Traci noticed me in them. Traci showed me and that was how we knew that we knew each other before. That has always been our link to each other, we were Crum Kids. We both have had friends over the years and lost touch a little while there, but always find our way back to each other. I honestly don't know what I would do without her. She has always been my Jiminy Cricket. She has always been the voice in my head, the one that I go to when I have hard decisions and she is always there, loving, supporting and encouraging me; no matter what.

What is more valuable to me is that she is always honest with me, even when I don't want to hear the truth. She is that person that will hold up a mirror to your face and say look at what you are becoming, do you like that person, if not, change her. A lot of the startling reality checks are vital and some are welcome while others teach me grace and patience, but there are always the ones that you don't want shown to you. But, she does it so lovingly and delicately, that you almost thank her for telling you that you are being a ridiculous bitch, and you hang up going, "wow, how does she do that?" I don't know how she does it, but I have always envied her for that. She is vocal and is never afraid to say what she means when she needs to say it. She oozes confidence within our friendship and within herself to be able to do this and never worry about our relationship. With her there is no need for a, "please don't take this the wrong way", because I always know everything is done with love and in the full intent of making me a better person. Without her, I am less than. I am a shell.

One day we were talking and reminiscing as we tend to do from time to time. This is generally when we gossip about some ridiculous memory from our younger years and still find it particularly hilarious. This was the day that she told me she thought that we were "soul sisters". She thought that God had brought her and I together so that she could one day bring me back to God. After losing my mom, and being molested, I had no relationship with God. In fact I was incredibly angry with him for all I had endured. But, Traci has never given up on bringing me to God. That is what she has done over the years, ever so gently. She didn't run in guns blazing and yell, "go to church" and "worship!"

Instead, she asked me when I visited her if we could squeeze in church before I went home? Knowing I can never turn her down, off we went to her church, Eleven 22. She knew what she was doing, she knew that it was what I needed and she was confident that this was the right time for me to accept Christ. I was extremely nervous, but she guided me in every step. We signed our children in and went to get a seat with her husband. Before too long, I was changed. This place that I had steered clear of for so many years, had made me feel so welcome and safe. I listened to Pastor Jobi talk, and I honestly am not gonna lie and say I remember anything he said specifically, but it was how he said it that resonated with me. What I do remember though, is exactly how I felt. I cried. I felt safe. I felt listened to. I felt strong. I felt like I was where I was supposed to be at that moment.

Wiping my tears away, Traci looked at me and said, "God spoke to you today." And I believed her. I couldn't understand how I was so moved by a man's words and song, but I was. I started to gently ask Traci questions about the bible and asking her to explain certain things to me that seemed confusing. She became my spiritual guide and guided me to God. Now, we talk on a daily basis, and God is in my heart and in my corner showing up for me every day. That same cynical young lady that sat in a church discussing unspeakable acts and asking how God could let them happen to me, now knows that I am perfectly made in his eyes and he has laid out my journey, I just have to have faith, let go and enjoy the ride. I don't question things as much as I did before because I know he is guiding them and I am just walking along the path he paved for me. I am loveable again and always have been.

Without me even knowing it, over time, she became my conscience. She became the voice in my head pushing me to be my best. She became my best friend out there under the flourescent lights of Southwood Middle School life. Somehow, I was blessed that day at United Methodist when I became a Crum Kid and Traci became my soul sister. Every person in this world needs a Traci. Someone that no matter how ridiculous you become, or how misguided, they remain in your corner and stay loving you. Karen and Don, my hat goes off to you and I thank you for Traci, my best friend, my Jiminy Cricket. I must've done something right in a previous life, because I have been blessed with Traci.

Samantha

Samantha has always been there, from my first memories as a child and in old birthday photos. Her mom is the sister of my mom's brother's wife; so yeah, she's basically my sister. For the past 20+ years, she has been my rock, my person, my sister and some days my mother. She has guided me, shown me right from wrong and taught me how to be a better woman, friend and mom; without even realizing it. I am sure my besties are not surprised that I feel this way and so strongly for them and their influences in my life, but they hate every minute of it! My people are not mushy like me. I am a word person, they are action people. I like words, I like using them in sentences dripping and oozing with feelings of admiration and love. I like saying them out loud for all to hear. My besties are more internal and I am a largely external introvert. That is the compliment between us all. They just don't use the words. But what they use is their actions. If I was ill, scared or hurt, they would drop everything to be by my side; even when I didn't realize I needed them. They are there, like a trusty sidekick that just always seems to pop up when you need them. They seem to call just at the right moments and plan trips when my life is falling apart; which tends to unfortunately be, often.

Back to Samantha. I showed up at 17 pregnant, scared, bruised and battered to my Aunt and Uncle's house in Ft Lauderdale. Samantha and her now husband, then boyfriend Mario come in while we are eating dinner. I hadn't seen Samantha in years, maybe since my mom died, but she was exactly the same. Samantha is that cousin that you looked up to. She was a cheerleader, and she had the most beautiful almost turquoise blue eyes and always had great hair. She perfected the 80's and early 90's Aquanet Wave, and it was like her signature style. She comes running in and has to use the bathroom, and yells "you got spray in here Mindy?" While she was away in the bathroom, I met her Mario. This is the man who would be her husband and father to her children. She comes out, sits down and welcomes me right in. It was as if no time had passed. She asked me if I wanted to go out with her and her friends and I was happy to spend time with her. From that moment, we were inseparable. We have always remained constant in each other's lives, even when we were angry with each other.

She is my person. The person. She is godmother to my eldest and has not only been there for me, but seen me at my absolute worst and stuck around. I seem to suffer from bouts of depression that I have always ignored and never admitted to. Shortly after my 25th birthday, it reared it's seemingly unpleasant head and hit me like one of those ACME anvils in the cartoons; it flattened me, it engulfed me. We had gone out for my birthday and I spent the night at her house. That morning I woke up and was overwhelmed with thoughts of failure. You see, days before, my father had told me what an ungrateful selfish child I was because I didn't drive down to Miami to spend Christmas with him and instead stayed home in Fort Lauderdale with my extended family. What he didn't realize or consider was that Kayla and I both felt more at home in Ft. Lauderdale than we ever had in Miami. But he took it as me not wanting to be with him for the holiday and decided to verbally attack me, demean me and my character as a consolation prize. I felt worthless and awful, but continued on with the festivities for my kid and everyone else's benefit. But those feelings came back, hard a few days later. Anyhow, I went home, put Kayla down for a nap and found my mom's box. Anyone that has lost someone vital to their life, has a box. This box contained all that was left of my mom. Her things, her memories and memories of her. Everything but her voice, touch or smell was in that box. The University of Miami keychain that was always on her keys, so 80's and so memorable and at a quick glance was a deadly object. It was like this clear brick of dominance, much like The U and extremely worthy of the UM swag fans know and love. My mom began my love affair with The Miami Hurricanes when I was very little and it has remained with me since then. So this minor item is a priceless treasure, and I will never let it go. Her driver's license and those terrible papers from Jackson Memorial's Heart Transplant squad, telling of her recovery and steps to keep this new heart. The photos that take your breath away and make you feel like a Mack Truck just ran you over. The memories from a seemingly happy childhood, a front for all to see. I slowly went through each item, reveling in the memories, challenging myself to remember each one. The tears flowed down my cheek and onto the box and then I was drowning, suffocating deep in that same depression I had denied for so long. I wanted my mom, I needed my mom and these memories emanated molestation and abuse. But, she was nowhere I could get to. So, in an insane moment, my damaged and broken mind told me to take every pill in my house and join her.

Now, depression is a hideous beast that rears its ugly head at the most inopportune times, this being one of them. I convinced myself that Kayla would be better off without me and that Samantha and Traci did not need me anymore. I convinced myself that all the pain I had endured to date was enough and I could not endure anymore. I convinced myself that God didn't love me or care for me and that was why I had endured all I had. I convinced myself that this, ending my life, was the only answer. There's that dominant bitch, depression, and she is an evil bitch. She has a way of making you believe that everyone that loves you would be fine if you left and your pain was more important than how you made others feel in this world. That the ones you love, will love or have not met yet would be better off without you in their life. Depression is a selfish and egotistical bitch.

I swallowed so many pills; I couldn't count them all and some wouldn't go down. I called Samantha and asked her to come get Kayla. The rest from there is, hazy, that is the only word I can use. It was as if time slowed down. I watched my cousin cry and saw the disappointment in her eyes looking at me lying on the floor carrying my 6 year old sleeping precious child in her arms out the door. She ran with my child knowing that she should have never seen her mother that way, and trying to get her out before any police came and took her from me. Kayla did not know anything, still to this day, until this section of my life, she does not know that this happened. I laid on that floor wishing I would die, with my cousin's husband kneeling next to me, trying to save me. I believe there was some CPR and screams, maybe, but we just don't talk about it. I hurt so many people that day, lost in my own grief, selfishness, thoughts and feelings. I will never forget how Samantha looked at me and how Mario stayed with me. I will never forget that if it wasn't for God, my daughter wouldn't have her mother.

The guilt of that day has hung with me for all these years. The disappointment and pain in Samantha's eyes is something I never wanted to see again. From there, I went to the hospital by ambulance where they pumped my stomach and I watched charcoal shoot out of my mouth and burn my nose. They admitted me on a Baker Act and I was sent to the Psych Ward for days. No contact with my child or my cousin or the outside world. I sat in disbelief and disappointment in myself, depressed and overwhelmed with what I had tried to do. The sounds of mentally ill people screaming throughout the night and day was overwhelming. I knew if I had to stay there any longer, I was going to be completely insane. So, I conformed and embraced the multiple group therapy sessions everyday so I could pass the time on my 72 hour hold. I went home about three days later, Samantha picked me up, with my sweet Kayla. I have never seen her look at me that way, that day, since then. I scared her. I tried to take the easy way out and didn't think of the path of pain I would have left behind me; I gave up. God had a different plan for me and I was still here to live and make it up to Kayla and her everyday.

From that day on, I promised her and myself I would never do that again. I promised that I would always reach out to her if I felt that dark again. As I sit here writing this, I had another dark time and was barely making it through; and I reached out to her. I felt that fear washing over me. I felt that everything I was dealing with, I wasn't really dealing with and I needed help. This time, I found a therapist that I trusted and EMDR. This time, I didn't try and make a permanent decision to a temporary problem that I could talk through, with help, understanding, acceptance and guidance. I spent weeks crying and not eating. I didn't sleep and honestly have no clue how I didn't lose my job. It turns out that always stuffing the fears and emotions down inside of you will actually eat you alive. Actually facing them takes real courage and strength and you can't do it alone. I never really let myself grieve the loss of Massimo in my life, and I wore that pain like my own skin. No, he wasn't dead, he was just no longer mine. I had for months, pushed my feelings away and just walked through my life waiting for him to come back.

I am never alone when I have Samantha. As you already know, Samantha is my mom's brother's wife's sister's daughter. Mouth full, huh!? She is much more than a mouthful of words. She is where my strength comes from. She is where my adventure, yes for those that know me, I can be adventurous, comes from. She is where I find the strength and confidence to take on the world everyday. Samantha is so much more than my cousin, my bestie, my person,she is the sister I chose and the one that chose me. The one that I would have wanted from the start and the one I actually needed. Ironically, as a baby, my sister and Samantha looked like twins; so, I'm sorry Lizy, but we were never really good to each other and Samantha has never been anything but good to me.

While I write this, I am still overwhelmed by the need to not wound some people and censor myself. But, I made a promise to myself when I decided to really finally sit down and write this book that I had to be true to how I felt and what happened or I would never do it. So, if you are bruised by reading something about yourself here, that pain belongs to you, you can pack it up in a perfect little box. I don't need, want or own it, any longer and I don't make excuses for how I feel or how you take the information. I have spent years caring what everyone else thinks instead of being me and worrying about myself. That ends right here at this moment. If you are hurt, it is because you hurt me and never wanted to admit your part in it and in turn placed all the blame on me instead of owning up to your own dismantling of our relationship.

When I think about my two best friends, I am reminded that there is *some* good in me, because of them. That I *am* lovable and loved, because they show me that every day. They both, together and separately, make me a better human in different ways. They both love me, the real me, the one that most never see. The unfiltered, sometimes bitch and kind woman I have become. They have accepted me for me, always, unconditionally. I have never had to be anything but me for them to love and that kind of feeling is powerful all in its own right. I have not had the easiest life, but I have always had them; in my corner, cheering me on and supporting me.

I know you both well enough to know that this little section and book has made you proud, uncomfortable and happy all at the same time; I thank you for being you and for never leaving me. I thank you for loving me so unselfishly and wholeheartedly while others were conditional. I thank you for always encouraging me to strive for my dreams and accomplish them; and then celebrate with me as I conquer those dreams. You have taught me that I am, in fact, worthy of love and happiness. For a very long time and while I write this, I continue to struggle with the worthiness of any of that. But, you two tend to gently and sometimes forcefully remind and guide me to that exact thing. I am worthy. I must continue repeating that. Through the years, I have made friends, some have been seasonal and others like an octopus stuck to my face.

Shawn

The male penguin in my life, Shawn, didn't start out that way. As 5 year old's we met, while our brothers played baseball. He was this messy boy with long blonde hair and always dirty, but always inclusive of me. He never really has had a bad word for me or said one to me. We played on those fields together for years while our brothers played ball and our parents watched. Shawn grew on me, quick, and I began to look forward to baseball season because Shawn came with it. I was struggling with all my brother was doing to me and unable to talk about it, but with Shawn, I could be a normal kid; I could be me. He pushed me on the swings and we ran through the park chasing each other year after year.

After my dad and mom got divorced, my brother was on this traveling baseball team in the summer. I was ten at that time and his team was going to Puerto Rico that summer. My mom told my dad that I deserved to go since we were going to the country I came from. So, off we went to Puerto Rico for ten days, I was so completely thrilled to see where I came from. We got to the airport and I realized we were going on an airplane and I had never been on one. I was extremely nervous, but my mom was there next to me, so I felt secure. We board the plane and this warm flight attendant sees my trepidation and tries to make me feel better. She hands me a pair of wings and says if I am good, I will get to meet the pilot when we land. Challenge accepted! Good girl, party of one, those wings are mine!

I knew for sure that nothing would be able to surpass me getting to meet the pilot, so I tried my best to not scream, or misbehave. But, no one told me about turbulence. That shit is not for the faint at heart, especially a young impressionable heart. We were flying to the Caribbean during Hurricane season and there was a tropical disturbance out there so it was incredibly bumpy. I thought I was going to vomit. I chewed the gum my mom gave me so my ears didn't clog up, very intently and melodically and then held on for dear life. We landed safely in magnificent Puerto Rico, and I think I finally exhaled. I hopped up, excited to meet the pilot and the flight attendant said he's over there, you can shake his hand. I walked up, and was star struck, stuck out my hand and shook his rather large hand. Then I asked him, "you couldn't have done anything about the bumpy ride?" My mom was mortified. She ushered me along and thanked the pilot. The flight crew chuckled behind me. I've always had the ability to say the most inappropriate thing at the most inopportune time. Why should flying be any different?

We got into a cab to take us to the Hotel Intercontinental, a Waldorf Astoria hotel, look it up, that place is unreal and worth every single penny! There was so much to see, I kept turning around and looking out every window in awe of my country, my homeland, where I came from. We settled in and went to the pool. Well, this hotel had ten pools! I was in absolute heaven. While walking back to the pool, I ran into Shawn and his family. That same boy I played with for so many years, looked much cuter to me now. I couldn't understand it. I didn't look at him as the dirty boy that pushed me on the swings and played in the orange clay with me. Now, he was cute and not dirty. I couldn't understand how I could look at my friend Shawn like he was not a friend, but someone I wanted to hold hands with and maybe kiss.

We hung out there every chance we could. We swam and played video games and went in the hot tub. I felt so grown up doing all these big girl things while I was so small. On our last night there, Shawn and I were playing in the pool and he got out and went in to play the grab game in the gameroom. I was still swimming and he yelled to me to come there. I ran over, soaking wet and watched Shawn play the grab game. He was trying for this stuffed animal that had two bears holding a heart together and it said, "I love you". Shawn won that bear, and handed it right to me and told me he loved me that day. Yep, I was ten and so was he. I was on cloud nine. Shawn Bartlett loved me! What! Suck it haters!

Every girl at cheerleading would be so jealous now. You see, Shawn and I over the years had started seeing more of each other when I started cheerleading at Suniland. Shawn played football there and now my brothers were too. So we had baseball in the spring and football in the fall together. That trip changed me in so many ways. Being in my homeland learning about the history and witnessing the true beauty that is Puerto Rico was life changing. Shawn telling me he loved me was life changing. For the next few years, we did this on again off again dance. He would be someone elses boyfriend and I would be someone elses girlfriend and then we would always end up back together.

At Suniland, I had a boyfriend named Dwayne. He was the only person at the time that drew my attention away from Shawn. Dwayne has this older brother, Darren, that over the years has become a very treasured friend, but at the time he was just so cool to me. Dwayne began my lifelong issues with boys and then unattainable men. You see, Dwayne didn't want to be my boyfriend. But, I persisted, Darren's warnings and all. I would change him. I would get him to only want me. He had this suave look about him when he took his sweaty helmet off. Tall, muscular and handsome. He was like a greek god on the football field. Everyone knew his name and I was his girl, I had changed him and he wanted me. I felt so awesome, but continued to look for Shawn on the field and wanted to see him. Dwayne and I broke up, in what I am sure was some teenage dramatic fashion and Shawn was there. He was always there. We got back together, again. Dwayne wanted to make out with me and the thought of someone's tongue in my mouth grossed me out. But Shawn was ok waiting until I was ready.

The next year, football season began, Shawn was dating my friend Amanda. I was mortified. She talked about her new boyfriend so adoringly, like teenage girls do and I didn't know it was MY Shawn. She said, when we go to cheerleading practice, I will introduce you to him. She then talked about how cute he was and his beautiful blue eyes. So, I am excited to meet her new beau. We hop out of her father's car, Amanda's dad was the best car pool I ever had. He sang oldies in the car and we had the best time with him. Rest in peace Mr. Hathaway, thank you for always making me feel welcome and showing me what I wish my dad was like then.

Anyway, we hop out and start to walk around. Amanda runs off and comes back with no boyfriend. But, a few seconds later, around the corner comes Shawn. Sweaty, in that god awful orange jersey, holding his helmet. He looked like a handsome man in a marketing ad. He walked around that corner and I ran into his arms, like it was breathing. Amanda was dumbfounded. How did I know *her* boyfriend? She looked at me, and said is this the Shawn you always talk about? I nodded. He was the Shawn I *always* talked about. He was my Shawn.

I was getting stares from another football player at the time, so I walked away and talked with him. Charles' hot damn' Collier. This boy was unlike any other boy. Built like a man with a chiseled smile that could melt stone and beautiful teeth. I think he is the reason I am obsessed with dating a man with good teeth. He had the best support team in his family. His mama was always looking super fly in the stands and step dad, Jasonos, was so nice to me. I finally had a boy that wanted me as much as I wanted him and it felt magnificent. Charles and I looked like some kind of Friday night lights poster. Him the star football player and me in my cheerleading outfit. He would throw his arm around my shoulders so I could hold his hand and we would walk off the field together; sometimes I even held his sweaty helmet for him. He was dreamy, respectful and handsome. But, what always stood out to me was how kind he was. He cared. He got it. He was a good guy. And, in my true nature, I fucked it up. I don't know how he and I are still friends, and how he doesn't hate me; but he doesn't. He was a great boyfriend then, I was trash to him. Charles was the first boy I brought home. My dad LOVED him and my dad liked no one.

He came over for dinner one night and was so polite, my mouth dropped. That was when he gave me his name plate. Every 90's kid knows how valuable this moment is. It was the 90's equivalent to the 50's letterman jacket. It was relationship goals and teen love all rolled into a gold chain around my neck bearing his name and a "Taken" charm to tangle as well. True gentlemen shit with him, always, his mother would be so proud of the boy he was then. He held my hand every time we were together, and I loved it, I felt safe. He kissed me softly, no tongue, because I wasn't ready for that, and was always respectful to me. But, I wanted Shawn and Amanda had him. But, I think Shawn always wanted me too. They broke up and we were back on almost instantly. That was the year we finally got to hang out outside of our brother's baseball games and our football games. We got to actually hang out together, alone.

So, Shawn and I could finally "date". He came to my house and watched movies and swam in the pool with me. We went on walks through the neighborhood and one night in particular stands out to me the most. We were watching Beauty and the Beast in my living room. I laid my head on his lap, he stroked my hair. Weeks prior to that, I had talked to my step mother about kissing and using the tongue. EW. But, she told me that I would know what to do when it happened if I saved it for the right boy and he would wait until I was ready. I can't help but think that there was SO much more in that statement than kissing. Anyhow, Belle was being a total turd and Shawn and I are enjoying the movie. I looked up at him and he smiled at me, his blue eyes twinkled a little in the recessed lighting and then he did it. He leaned in and touched my face so gently, so soft and deliciously sweet and then went in for our first real kiss, with tongue! WHAT! He knew me well enough to know I was ready without ever telling him. He waited for me and this was just my first kiss, not even sex, and he made it not only memorable, but perfect. It was like a movie. Soft, tender, loving and slow. He ran his fingers through my hair and put his hand on my face the way they do in movies and on TV. I was in awe. He was smooth and suave for a teen. It was as if time stood still and the whole world was circling us. It was the best moment of my childhood and the most memorable. He gave me his beeper that night, 90s kids rejoice! It was clear and had a gold tacky ass chain on it. My parents were super strict and we wanted to be able to keep in touch and I was literally grounded *all* the time! I had to keep that beeper hidden, my dad wasn't having it. "Only pimps and drug dealers have beepers" was what he said, to which I replied, "which one are you then?" Yeah, that response didn't go over well and got me grounded for a few months.

We beeped each other all the time. You see that was the best thing back then for grounded kids. You dialed quickly and sent your little message and hung up; parents had no clue. We got creative in how we communicated that way. But most messages were 143 (I Love you) and 823 (Thinking of you). We would arrange to meet at the park when I was grounded because exercise was the only thing I was allowed to do. We would walk around the park hand in hand and just be happy in the same park he pushed me on the same swings from our younger years. We had come full circle. I knew we would be in love forever.

The next summer, Shawn's dad took a job with AT&T (AKA Bellsouth) in Daytona Beach and he was moving away. I was crushed and heart broken. We had finally been given a real chance to be together. We had shared so much and now he was leaving me. That was the worst summer of my life. Shawn left and my mom died in the same month. Poor Shawn was trying to take care of me from so far away and be my friend, it was impossible because I wouldn't let him. I wouldn't let anyone, but I will elaborate more later. He showed up at my house in September around his birthday, because our High Schools were playing each other and they were a HUGE rivalry, so he came in for the game. I remember my doorbell ringing, and I went to answer it and before I could open it, I saw him in the glass. I thought I was dreaming! I longed to open my front door to his handsome face and warm smile, I dreamt of it nightly after he left; and here he was making my dreams come true. I opened the door and jumped into his arms. I didn't even care that we were broken up. He was here for me. We stood outside talking and catching up, leaning up against his car. He looked so different to me that day, he looked more mature, but he was still my Shawn. Handsome, kind and considerate; and my friend when I needed one. He wanted me to come to the game with him, but my wicked step mother said I couldn't. When he was leaving, he held me tight and told me how sorry he was about my mom and that he wasn't there to help me and kissed me on my forehead and left. That moment right there, I knew we would always be in each other's lives and I knew he would always love me.

Over the years, Shawn and I always stayed in touch. We even tried to get back together sometime in our early twenties. The defining moment in our love affair turning to friendship was one night when we were about twenty-one. Shawn was in town for work, he was now working for AT&T like his dad. I HAD to see him. He had always been this unattainable relationship to me. I was convinced if we had a real chance, we would be together forever. So, we went out. Him, a coworker, my girlfriend Mandy and I. After partying at Baja, Mandy and I's favorite spot, where I tried to entice Shawn by dancing on the bar, we went home to my house. The next night, we went out just the two of us, like a real date, but with my 3 year old tagging along. We went back to my house, I put Kayla to bed and then we snuggled on the couch and kissed. It was as I remembered sitting in my parents living room so many years before watching Beauty and The Beast. Shawn and I never had a problem kissing, it was always perfection. He taught me how to kiss. So for all you men and boys I have kissed since then, you have Shawn to thank for the little lip thing I do. Fun fact, Shawn can tell you the movie we were watching too, real shit. He is that kind of guy, the one that remembers all the little insignificant things that actually matter.

We decided to head to the bedroom. I took his hand in mine and led him, where we kissed more and he began to undress me. My mind was racing and screaming, "OH MY GOD, SHAWN IS UNDRESSING ME!!" We laid on my bed and kissed while he got on top of me. In that moment, my entire childhood flashed before my face, the park days, the football days, that last time we saw each other at my house; and I started to snort. He looked at me trying to not laugh and began to snort too and then this symphony of laughter broke out between us. All while his penis was just strategically inside of me and the two of us were laughing so hard that it slipped out. We had reached that point. That

point where there is no going back. We were friends, good ones at that and we would never be more. He is my best guy friend. He has seen me through so much hurt and happiness that I would be lost without him. He is my guy. He is that guy that you know you can count on for the rest of your life. So, in reality, I do get to love him forever, just in a different way. Every guy is measured against how Shawn has made me feel over the years.

We are all grown up now. We've got kids and divorces under our belts and happiness too. He is special to me in a way that no other man will be. He is my Shawn. He is my best friend and some of my fondest memories lay in his pretty blues. We have moved past any romantic attachments and on to something deeper and more meaningful, lifelong friendship. I feel like the luckiest girl in the world when it comes to Shawn. I could have lost him forever many moons ago, but God felt that we needed to remain in each other's lives. Who knows why, but I don't question it, I embrace it.

Brandon, My "B"

In October 2015, I was going on vacation to Cocoa Beach, with an old friend Karie and her friend Brandon. I called Shawn and told him that he should come and meet us and spend the weekend with us since Cocoa wasn't far from Daytona Beach where he still lived. He agreed, and the plans were made. Karie, Brandon and I began the drive from North Carolina to Cocoa Beach. Cocoa was special to me, my dad's father lived there when I was growing up and the Kennedy Space Center is there and I loved that place. My grandfather took us there in my childhood and I fell in love with the place. Anyhow, on this drive to Cocoa, Brandon and I start to get to know each other. Karie was entangled with him and he was off limits in my mind since they were essentially on this vacation together. But, Brandon and I became friends on that trip and when Shawn arrived, they became instant friends. I thought this was too good to be true, my best friend Shawn is on vacation with me and now I have this new friend Brandon who was so amazing in his own right and a real gentleman.

Shawn and Brandon bonded over their love of football, specifically the Miami Dolphins and Mexican Word of the Day memes. Shawn and I were huge UM and Dolphin fans, and to hear that Brandon was too, was remarkable to me. The vacation was great, and like all great things, it had to end. Brandon, Karie and I drove home and Shawn went back to his house. Brandon and I exchanged phone numbers and Shawn and he did too. We would all FaceBook message each other memes, Dolphins updates or just simple hello's. By November, Brandon and I were texting regularly, but just memes and football stuff. Karie became incredibly jealous of the relationship Brandon and I had formed and questioned my loyalty to her friendship and my motives with Brandon's friendship. I had no interest in Brandon romantically, I just enjoyed talking to someone that had similar interests as I did. Karie stopped being my friend because her anger towards our friendship was more important than the actual truth. When everything went down with Karie, I turned to Brandon for comfort, clarity and understanding since he knew Karie longer than I had. Brandon was there, he listened and offered a shoulder to cry on and understood how difficult it was for me since Karie and I lived in the same apartment building.

Before I knew it, we spoke regularly and at length and he always made time for me. He encouraged me and pushed me gently to be better. He listened to me talk to him about the many bad dates I had been on and offered the male perspective. Karie and I became "friends" again and she was in another relationship with this guy she met shortly after she accused Brandon and I of doing things behind her back. We found ourselves at Brandon's house one night and she shamelessly flirted with him, while he looked at me extremely uncomfortable. They had sex a few times during this period of time, not when I was around, so she told me. But she was in another relationship and Brandon didn't want to be with her romantically since she was in another relationship and essentially playing with two men's emotions. He would call me and we would talk about it and he would tell me how he didn't trust her and didn't want to be with her but she wouldn't take the hint. Then I had Karie telling me that she was in love with him and he wouldn't give her a chance. I was being pulled in two different directions and wasn't sure where my loyalty should lie, so I chose Brandon.

Karie had hurt me and Brandon cleaned that mess up, so my loyalty was with him. I kept what he told me to myself and let Karie continue her pleas to me to talk to him for her. I finally asked her, "If you are in love with Brandon, why are you in this other relationship?" I didn't believe that she loved him, I believe and still do believe that she loved the idea of Brandon and what he had to offer. He was a good man, with a great heart and a true gentleman and would do anything for you and to keep you safe if he cared for you. He is the perfect man. Karie couldn't tell me anything other than she didn't want to end the relationship she was in and take a chance that Brandon would be with her, so she stayed in her relationship living with another man. That told me that she did not love Brandon and it told me that she did not deserve Brandon. At this point, Brandon and I had become best friends, he called me his best friend and I felt he was mine. I felt lucky to have him in my life and as my best friend. Karie moved into a house she bought and the guy came with her, so again, I didn't think Brandon meant what he said he did to her and my true loyalty lies within him, but I enjoyed being friends with her.

Brandon and I began talking more and more at this point and I needed some work done on my car, and since he is a mechanic he told me he would do it for me. It was April 2018, and I got in my car and drove to him in Greensboro where he lives, about an hour and half away from me. It was chilly that day and I wore a gray shirt and white linen pants. He set a chair for me in his driveway and began working on my car. We talked and laughed and he showed me the car stuff he was doing and explained why he was doing each thing. At some point, I looked at him and saw him in a different light. He was not just Brandon, my Miami Dolphin loving friend, he was attractive and kind and I looked at him and began to wonder what a life with him would be like. I was baffled that he looked different to me that day and almost in shock too. He told me he had to drive my car to make sure it was good and wanted to give it a wash. He opened the passenger door for me and let me in my car and then drove us around Greensboro. He showed me places he liked to eat at and the church he attended and then we pulled into a car wash. He began to wash my car, and smiled at me and asked if I wanted to get out while he washed it. I agreed and before I could put my feet on the ground he swept me up off them.

He didn't want my white pants to get wet and I had flip flops on so he was trying to keep my feet dry. That's what I told myself at least. I watched this man that was my friend, my best friend, clean my car with care and precision and smile at me. I walked over to him and hugged him to say thank you, and this hug was a different hug than ones of the past. It was warmer, longer and intimate. I shook it off and he carried me back to the car and put me in, now he could have driven it forward, but he carried me again. That stuck in my mind. We went to grab some lunch and he took me to one of his favorite spots and wouldn't let me pay, open a door or pull out my chair. Being with Brandon and in his presence, you get a crash course in how a lady should be treated; in what a gentleman is. We drove back to his house and I got another long hug and I thought he was going to kiss me, and I left headed back home. The entire drive I analyzed everything about that day and couldn't believe I had been storing feelings for him that had just come out.

Karie was fun and gave me a confidence back that had been gone for many years. My fortieth birthday came around and Traci, my dear friend Lauren and Karie were taking me to Savannah. I was ecstatic, I had never been and I was turning forty! Karie backed out the night before because she had decided to have her IUD removed two days before the trip and she was in pain. She was furious with me that I still insisted that she pay her share of the hotel room, since we were all staying in one room. Why should the rest of us have to cover the cost for her since she backed out last minute? A hotel would have charged her if she booked it herself and canceled, so I thought she should still pay. She decided that I was a shitty friend and she once again was done with being my friend. Brandon was not surprised and angry with her for how she treated me and upset with me that I even allowed her back in my life in the first place. Over the next couple years, Brandon would work on my car whenever it needed an oil change, tires, anything I would drive to him and see him. Before I knew it, I was looking forward to these visits and was excited for them. My kids loved Brandon and encouraged me to tell him how I felt. I would brush them off and not believe that I should. It was December 2020, and I went to see him for an oil change and told him I was going to Tennessee to see Kayla the day after Christmas and asked him if he wanted to come with me. He did, to my surprise. He came on Christmas night and spent the night at my house and in my bed and nothing happened. We got up the next day and drove to Kayla. I took the car drive as an opportunity to see what he liked in a woman and what he looked for to see if I was even his type. He told me he was attracted to strong women, that made their family a priority and someone that could make him laugh, feel safe and enjoy sports with. Um...he just described me.

That night we slept in the same bed together in the hotel room again and when I was starting to fall asleep, I felt him attempt to put his arm across me and then whisper to himself. "No." We woke up the next morning and it was my birthday. We laid in bed together and talked. It was the best talk we had and it was nothing deep or special, it was just us being ourselves and talking. I asked him, "Brandon, have you ever looked at me as anything but a friend?" I figured this was my shot to find out if my feelings for the last two years were one sided and I held my breath while waiting for his answer. He quickly responded, "no." I got up and said, "oh, ok, I am going to get in the shower." I went in the bathroom and cried and was so mad that I may have ruined my friendship with him over one-sided feelings.

We drove to meet Kayla for brunch and he again, was Brandon, a gentleman, opening my door, and pulling out my chair. At one point I had left something in the car for Kayla and he went out with me to get it because he didn't want me going alone in a strange place, and I almost fell on the snow and ice and he caught me and it was so safe and comfortable. We left the restaurant, said our goodbyes and headed home. I didn't talk about feelings or anything, I just wanted him to hold my hand, I remember that longing feeling. Brandon dropped Riley and I at home, carried our bags in and gave us both hugs and headed home to his house. Twenty minutes later, my phone rang and it was him. "Why did you ask me that this morning when we were laying in bed?" I knew what he was asking, but I wanted him to tell me, so I said, "asked you what?" He said, "if I ever looked at you as anything more than a friend." I knew this was my only chance and I took it. I told him, "because I have feelings for you and I have for two years." He exhaled hard, and I thought to myself, "oh shit this is bad." He softly said, "I lied this morning." I don't know if I have ever smiled that big, but I smiled. We talked the rest of the way home trying to figure out how we could be together or at least see if there was something there to be together.

Karie and I were friends again at this point and I was feeling guilty that she didn't know that Brandon had gone with me to Tennessee, so I went to her work with the sole purpose of telling her and I chickened out. Instead, I lied when she asked me if Riley and I went alone. I left her work and drove home and I felt sick that I lied to her, so I texted her and told her that I lied and I was sorry and Brandon had come with us. She somehow knew he did and accused Brandon and I of having sex for years behind her back, which had never happened. We had not done anything but hug each other and steal glances at each other. I called Brandon and told him and she was texting him at the same time. He told me he knew she would respond that way and he was sorry she had, but she had no chance with him and he wanted me.

Man did that feel amazing!

He blocked her phone number and we started talking daily and planned out our first date. It was January 23, 2021 and Brandon and I went to my favorite Mexican restaurant. He had driven over and was staying at my house again and I was in awe. I got to wake up with him again. At dinner, he was a gentleman as always and looked so handsome and smelled so good. He told me how beautiful I looked, not hot, not sexy, beautiful. We decided to be together that night and we went back to my house, got in my bed and watched the UFC fight that was on that night. We snuggled together and he didn't try anything at all. He just held me and I fell asleep in his arms while I made him watch Gilmore Girls after the fight ended. The next day, neither of us wanted to have him go. We laid in bed all day and talked and watched movies and ate with Riley. It was beautiful. It became 7pm and he had to head home since his drive was an hour and a half, and he held me, and lifted my chin up, and kissed me, softly and smooth. My whole body instantly felt warm, loved and safe. I walked him out and again he hugged me, but this time, he did that one thing a man can do that will steal my heart, he picked me up and I wrapped my legs around his waist. He kissed me again and this time, it was romantic and life changing.

I don't know what the future holds for Brandon and I romantically or as friends, but in that moment, he was everything I had always wanted and more. Those are them, my penguins. The people that care more about me than I care about myself some days. They are the people that formed me and continue to. My besties. My people. My soul sisters. My sisters. My boys. My friends.

Chapter Nine

EMDR & PTSD Healing time

$\mathcal{Y}$ou know it's funny to me to write a chapter about friendships and how blessed I am with mine, while my step monster always said I had no solid relationships in my life. This woman is something else, she's as pleasant as spoiled milk. When I set out to write this book, I sat down with Traci and we mapped out some of the chapters together. I told her what I wanted to say and she told me, If you aren't ready to be raw and unfiltered, you can't do it yet. She was right, she's always right for that matter. I would love to say that my story has just flowed out of mind onto paper easily and effortlessly, but that would be a ginormous lie. I have in fact had to take several breaks from writing this and even had to seek out professional help just to process the trauma. I am incredibly grateful that I have my therapist, she is helping me heal with the use of EMDR therapy for PTSD. This is absolutely no joke, and I implore anyone with trauma to seek this type of specialist to help you cope. Now, this has not remotely been easy in therapy, it has forced me to face the images, feelings, smells and pain I hid from. My trauma is palpable, it is real, raw and life changing. But, I am healing in this hypnotic and exhausting world of EMDR. I have learned that everything that makes me who I am was and is because of that moment after childbirth when my birth mother gave me up. That moment changed me and traumatized my future in a home of disgusting circumstances.

You see, I thought after all these years later of what my fucktard brother did to me, I would be past it. But, sadly, I am not. I thought in the midst of church groups and therapy multiple times over the years that I would have been healed. I am not. I am not close. What I didn't realize was that I had to first heal from the most detrimental thing that could happen to a person in their childhood. This thing that stayed locked up deep and lost surfaced over a decade ago in a bout with insomnia and new parenthood again.

So it was 2007, early May. Riley, my precious baby, was mere weeks old and I was a new mom sleep deprived; we've all been there where you can't remember when your last shower was and if you even brushed your teeth that day. My ex-husband, Michael, worked and I stayed up with a crying baby. I was breastfeeding, so I thought it was only fair. Anyhow, I had gotten creative at this point because lack of sleep equals migraine for me, and I needed some sleep. I had Riley in her co-sleeper in our bed and we were all snuggled up until she woke up crying. In a sleep-deprived haze, I sat up, put her on my boob and partly fell in and out of sleep. It was so cold in the room and peaceful looking at her and listening to her suckling, I was content and happy and very sleepy. My ex-husband was actually not snoring that night, which was a miracle all on its own. I remember my hair was up in a messy bun and I was wearing an oversized pj shirt and my husband's boxer briefs. The room was silent and cold and all I heard was Riley's nursing sounds and cooing, it was tranquil.

All of a sudden, these visions and moments came running across the room like a kaleidoscope circling me. Fast at first and then micro slow and I could barely believe what was being shown in front of me. I could hardly stomach it. I took Riley off my breast and laid her down in the bed with her father and nudged him to tell him to take her and ran into the bathroom. I barely made it behind closed doors when the tears, fear and dirtiness washed over me. Those images I saw were so real, but could they have been? I sat on the floor in the bathroom, rocking and sobbing.

Clarity was washing over me. I remember counting the tiles and staring at my blue jean shower curtain that my ex-husband vomited all over in the beginning of us living together after a drunken night. I had wanted that shower curtain so bad, and his stupid vomit made me have to wash it and then it shrunk some and I was so mad at him for that. I remember sitting there getting overwhelmed. I couldn't breathe. I couldn't move.

Michael came in and I looked at him, tears running down my face. He said, "Riley needs you, what's wrong?" I remember saying the words, but not believing them. I remember how awful they tasted coming out of my mouth. I remember the look in his eyes. I was now, damaged to him. I was his wife, but I was no longer there. It was a young, little girl he wanted to help. He held me on that floor while I cried on him and repeated that phrase over and over.

My mom molested me.

I remember not wanting to touch Riley alone again. I remember being terrified I was infected with whatever sickness seemed to be around me and kept finding me. I remember not wanting to breastfeed her ever again, but also being heartbroken because our bond was so strong already and I didn't want to lose that. My ex-husband called the therapist we saw for marital problems the next morning and got me in really quick. I remember hearing him on the phone with her saying, she thinks her mom molested her and she won't touch Riley anymore. Michael and I had a lot of problems, but when the shit hits the fan, you want him in your corner. He is there for me when I need him, and during this time, when I need him the most. I can only imagine what his mind must have thought. I can only imagine what his heart must have felt. We have this new marriage, new baby and now a brand new sexual trauma. I feel that this played a part in our demise. Not only did I not want to touch Riley, I didn't want Michael to touch me. I was infected. I was damaged. I was spoiled. I was unworthy. I was, once again, dirty.

Over the next few months, memories were unlocked and dealt with that I was not ready to deal with. Vividly, I had the same vision over and over again and in my sleep. My mother is lying down on her bed pouring honey all over herself and making me lick it off. My brain won't let me go any further than that. My mind blocks the next moments from me still to this day. I have multiple visions of this and similar events that occured, but I get no further than that. My brain is protecting me, but I am just not sure from what. It is wretched enough though, wretched enough to completely fuck you up. I remember one time when I was maybe 5, she made me put her tampon in while she laid in the bathtub and shoved my tiny hand into her vagina. It was as disturbing and disgusting as it sounds and I am sure that no one could imagine this horror. She would make me "breastfeed" on her and used different liquids to entice me there and hold my head there. She couldn't have kids and I assume that this was her fucked up idea of getting the experience of breastfeeding, and I believe that is why in that vulnerable and exhausted sleep-deprived moment, my brain unlocked the trauma for me.

Part of my therapy was to bring Riley with me and we would try and breastfeed. At this point I was feeding her, but reluctantly. I wouldn't look at her and it was hard. She loved to stare at me and smile while running her fingers through my hair and squeezing my breast when she fed; I didn't pay it any mind, when before I would coo back to her. If she started, I stopped it, she must've been so confused. I was so afraid I was going to be like my mom and hurt my child. Fear is powerful and suffocating. I think Michael was afraid I was broken. I watched day in and day out my husband look at me like my dad did that day in the car on the way to my church group therapy. It was all too familiar that look and now my husband was searching for his wife much like my dad was looking for his grease monkey. I don't think I was ever the same again. I still don't feel the same.

But, with the therapist ever so gently guiding me back to bonding with my beautiful baby girl, I was able to enjoy feeding her and not feeling like it was sinful. I was able to allow her to stroke my hair and squeeze my breast without feeling dirty. I was able to be her mom despite what mine had done. The anger I felt would have to be dealt with someday, but I haven't been ready to, until now. It is more than that though, not just anger, it is betrayal I think. This woman took me into her home, cared for me, promised to protect me and keep me safe and the danger was in her own hands. She was the enemy, she was the scorpion in the family. She was the cancer, and I couldn't cut it out because it infected me.

This same woman that denied what Scott had done and then on her deathbed decided to come clean, she was wretched and she tainted her image in my head. I have spent years being so conflicted with love and anger and trying to forgive her. I have struggled with the demons she created within me. I have struggled with mourning her and loving her and despising what she did to me. You see, after my parents separated when I was in elementary school, my mom quit being a mom. She stopped cooking, cleaning and doing laundry. She went from Suzie homemaker to this shell that sat and didn't do anything anymore. My big brother would do that stuff now, we all would. She sat for weeks on end in a chair in the living room, crying, sobbing and mourning the loss of my dad and whatever part she played in it. My dad had fallen in love with Sandy, the wicked witch, my mom called her, and left us for her. He had this new life, new family, new home and son. He started a business and they moved into what my child-like self thought was a mansion. Five bedrooms, three bathrooms and a pool. We were able to get a pool! My mom was so distraught over that house and all its grandeur when she would drop us off there she would sigh. I always wondered if she was jealous that dad never was able to give them that kind of home, instead we lived in the heart of Perrine and not in a big fancy house.

During the time that my dad was creating his new life, my mom's life was falling apart. She took a photography job with one of those school portrait studios and she seemed happy. But something was off. My mom was traveling throughout Florida taking school portraits, we were even her models, it was like things were going back to normal; whatever that is. Then, it happened. We had to move in with dad and the wicked witch. My mom would come to see us in the beginning, and sneak to see me later on. She found loopholes in her own rules. She refused to even pull in the driveway of that house, so she would park on the street and lay on her horn. Slowly, she stopped coming by. My big brother had moved back with her rather quickly, and I am not one hundred percent positive that he ever really moved with us. He was mom's favorite, we all knew that, shit he knew that. My dad could never make him stay there, he was seventeen and worked and helped mom out.

My mom had a heart attack that year. It was bad. I remember seeing her and not really understanding what was going on, she just looked like she was dying. My brain is tricky sometimes and memories have been sent away to the vault of sorrow and I am not sure, but, I believe my step-mother came to that hospital with us to see my mom in the ICU. She needed a heart transplant. I have never felt like I understood all that transpired there, but somehow, a twenty five year old kid wrecked his motorcycle and my mom was able to get his heart. After the surgery, she had to take so much medicine. She was weak all the time and we did not speak. I was angry with her for not believing me about my disgusting brother and felt like she abandoned us. My wonderful step-mother likes to rehash the shit we write when we are children about our feelings, and decided to send me the letter of anger

I wrote to my mom shortly before she died, years later, expressing my anger that she didn't believe me about my brother. Like a great opportunist, they never miss their chance and she never does.

Anyone that knew my mom, and I mean anyone would tell you how important her children were to her. Some would say, we were her whole life. Every July 15, my heart stops for a second, my stomach hurts and I have a hard time functioning and thinking clearly. That is the day my mom died and ironically the day my "brother" was born. That was the day all my answers died and the day that the most important woman in my life left. That was the day that all the things that could help me grow as a person died. She died and took all my hope for any normalcy with her. She took the secrets of my birth parents, of what she had done to me and whatever else she had done, literally to her grave. What a thief.

She took away the opportunity to confront her for what she did to me and make her answer for it. She took away the opportunity to come clean to everyone about what she knew that Scott did to me. She took all that away. How could she? My mother. This woman that would do anything for her kids, destroyed me. Every year, that day sneaks up on me. It is difficult, but for different reasons. I mourn the life I should have had. I mourn the mom I deserved, not the one I got. I mourn my god damn vagina not being penetrated as a fucking toddler. With her passing, I lost all my hope to understand my pain. So, when I write on FaceBook that I miss my mom and I miss being able to see and talk to her, that is a fucking lie. I am angry that she left like a coward. I am angry that she was able to violate my childhood and god knows how many others' but was able to slide out unscathed and unconfronted while I have days that I can't function like a normal woman, whatever that is; how unjust and quite frankly, comical. It is to me the wrong kind of irony, if it even qualifies as irony. She was this woman with a Catholic heart and devoted her life to her children and the foster children she cared for and yet that same Catholic loving heart destroyed me. I always wondered why she never had me baptized and I wonder now if it was because she knew what she had been doing to me and I was tainted and impure.

She never had to own up to what she did. Even the day on her deathbed, she lay there telling me all these motherly things she wanted me to hear, selectively choosing to leave out the part when she violated me and my innocence. Where was the, I am sorry I molested you? Where was that declaration? Oh I know, it was hidden behind telling me what shit Sandy is and how I have to be a better mom than both of them to my children. As I write this, I feel the anger washing over my body and the animosity almost choking me and wrapping around me like a python about to annihilate it's prey. I have never quite made peace with all she did and just how deeply it affected me. I am a work in progress, currently, and quite honestly, habitually. In fact my therapist told me to take a book writing break until we delve into some of these things more, but I have always had a rebellious streak and think that writing is raw. Writing is real, and it should be done when emotions are raw and real. That is why this will work, so I think.

I imagine my mom felt like shit when she found out about my dad and Sandy. I imagine she felt somewhat like the Miranda Lambert song, More Like Her. I imagine it destroyed her. I watched it destroy her day in and day out.

Through my time in EMDR, I learned that my dad leaving and how my mom felt about it was not my burden to bear. I learned that the pain and agony I went through during my childhood was not something that defined me and I was actually able to review those melancholy memories that used to consume me. With the assistance of the hypnotic therapy that is EMDR, I was able to change the pain associated with each deplorable act of my mother and "brother;" well, the ones that my protector parts would enable me to.

What's funny about EMDR is that you think you can go in and unlock all these memories and tackle them one by one, but those protector parts of you and the firefighters of you have a different ideal. You have to get their permission to unlock something that has remained hidden. You need their 'ok' to decipher through the wretchedness and begin to heal and sometimes, they aren't so welcoming. Sometimes, they are downright adamant that you will not touch a memory unless they say so. EMDR is so fascinating in its own right. I would sit there, eyes shut, focusing on my breathing and see what "came up" that my mind and body wanted to discuss. I would focus on how my body felt with each memory and where the discomfort was and describe how it felt. Sometimes, it was like hot coals were in my throat and other times, it was like someone went into my intestines and was twisting them tightly. The body responds to trauma in many different ways and EMDR allowed me to explore that and exhausted me when I did.

I would drive home after a session, and call Traci and just cry to her about what I unlocked. The bitch about this therapy is that while it is extremely effective, it is only an hour a week. So what do you do with the other many hours in the week after you've unlocked something deplorable? You cry, you write and journal and you try to connect with those parts and put them at ease. One of my parts, little girl me, was the most heartbreaking one of them all. She was a toddler sometimes and others a small baby, but she was always innocent and begging to be held. I would grab her and hold her and she would nestle in my arms and coo. I was hugging my younger self and putting her pain at ease. She would hide in the corner of my back yard, by this big tree and our swing set. She was always dressed in this yellow checkered dress with a carrot on the the side of it and holding her knees and sobbing. Sometimes, she was in the swings and reaching for me to hold her. I would tell her I would protect her and to wait for me and I would be back next time and she would sob and beg me to stay. Those visions and memories were traumatic to me and Traci helped me process them each time. It was like she knew every Wednesday at 3pm, I would call and we would get me through whatever I just dealt with.

I have never understood why my dad cheated, and I don't really care to explore his reasoning or hear him out on it. I have never understood why he left us and chose Sandy and her son over us, and continues to decades later. This pain and uncertainty huddled around a need for being chosen, is the definitive reason as to why I have no relationships with men that seem to last. I choose unavailable men, purposely so that I can feel disappointment when they don't choose me. Let's explore the parade of men from my past that are no longer in my life, some still are, because I am awesome and even if they can't commit to me, they still want to be my friend.

Chapter Ten

A Different Kind of Abuse

*W*e've gone over Shawn, Dwayne and Charles, so let's

go right ahead and move on to the one person that fucked me up for other people, maybe just as bad as my mom and "brother" did. It is Junior year at Miami Palmetto Senior High School, where I have become a quote un quote rebellious teenager, according to my parental units. I played softball, was on the newspaper staff and was a pretty good student there. I did smoke a lot of weed and drink on the weekends, sneak out of my house, sneak boys into my room and crap, but I don't think most haven't done something rebellious in their childhood. At this particular point I was hanging out with Melinda, this super pretty cool girl that I had some fun times with. I met a bunch of people through her, Terrell being one of them. We hung out a few times and he never seemed to be in school, which was interesting to me. That year was super difficult for the family. That was the same year that my step-brother, James, almost died. You see, I hated Sandy, but I liked James. My high school had off campus lunch and we were all coming back to school rushing to beat the bell, when I saw James backing up his Trans-Am. This car was sweet, and James worked hard for it. He had previously bought a canary yellow 69 camaro that he was rebuilding and it got stolen and stripped, naturally my parents blamed me for it because I got blamed for everything. They actually thought I had people come to the house and steal his car because I was bored or was just that much of a bitch. I did not, let's let the record be set that it was not me.

Anyhow, back to the Trans-Am. James is backing in playing some loud crap music he listened to. He got out of the car, looking like a rockstar with his long flowing blonde hair and all black outfit. As he closed the door, I saw him stumble and then collapse. I ran over to him and he was out cold, his head was split open and he was bleeding bad. I picked his head up and put it on my lap, blood was everywhere now. My hands and white Bongo jeans were covered with blood and I was screaming to call 911, someone help him. Rescue got there pretty fast, and they worked on my brother. He had to be airlifted, he was in really bad shape. The bitch shows up, and of course blames me. She thinks I gave her precious prince drugs or something equally as bad. It was like a fucking movie. She had the balls to stand there and blame me with our school resource officer standing there listening to her berate me. The helicopter left and so did she, thank goodness. I could finally cry. I could finally feel the moment I just was a part of and the fear for my brother. I could stop pretending I wasn't hurt and that she didn't even thank me for staying with him. She told me I didn't deserve to know how he was, that it was a family matter. What a damn cunt and she wonders why I rebelled. She never welcomed me. See, satan was dressed as a Jewish fitness freak and had married my dad.

That was the final straw for me. I was done with this bitch and she would know it. Mind you, this is the same woman that had my house key taken away and changed the alarm code on me and didn't tell me.

She would make me sit on the patio in the Florida heat until she came home to let me in. She knew I got out of school at 2:15pm, but most days she would show up right before my dad got home around 4:30 or 5pm. She was hateful and exercised her power all while abusing me. The abuse she did was not the physical kind, but she did put her hands on me, her abuse was verbal and mental. She knew how to zone in on my insecurities and make me feel as small as an ant all while trying to carry my load. When she would finally come home, she would smugly open the back door for me, like I was a cat that had been begging to come in. She never spoke a word to me, or looked in my eyes, she just isolated me. This woman caused some fucked up issues for me, but she didn't care. In her words, I would respect her and I wasn't in her eyes. The fact that I didn't bash her head in daily should have shown her I had some level of respect for her.

The fact that I didn't break the french door glass every day, should have shown her. One day, I remember I pretended to be asleep on my dad's reading chair on the patio and she came in and went to the kitchen, then to her bedroom, then back to the kitchen and began cooking dinner. She left me out there for another thirty fucking minutes. The day I ran away from home was one of these horrible days where she left me on the patio for hours.

It was February, and we got into the minute she opened the door for me. I had had absolutely enough. We argued and I told her I was leaving, she said good, but you can't take anything I bought you. Well, blow me down, I don't own shit, so I was leaving naked then I assume. She busted in my room and tried to take my radio from me. I was livid.

Any kid growing up in the 80's or 90's knows just how vital a boombox is. This is where you listen to the Power Love hour and the booty music we treasured and this bitch was trying to take it from me. We struggled over it and the struggle made it down the hallway to her bedroom where she was storing other things she busted in and took at this point. We were standing in her doorway, both fuming with anger and aggression. I looked at her, very plainly and seriously said, "How does it feel to know all the working out you do, all the hours in the gym and you still can't over power a child? You are weak."

I felt amazing, I felt untouchable in that moment. I felt like I was finally strong enough to break her toxic grasp. I let go and she stumbled backwards. I ran, and ran hard trying to get out of that hell hole. Every door I went to she pushed me away from. This was the same woman that didn't want me and now she is trying to be refrigerator Perry over here trucking me to make me stay; talk about confusing. I jumped over the cat gate and out the back door I went, barefoot and free. I never ran so hard in my life. I felt like Olivia Pope in the scene where she is captured and runs for her life. The wind was hitting my face and my feet were getting cut up but I was free. I heard her yelling something but didn't care, I pressed on to Traci's house; my safe place.

I got to Traci's and told her and her mom what had all happened. Her mom said you need to go home, I was not going back there I told her, respectfully. She made me promise that I would call my parents and tell them where I was and that I was safe. I called and they didn't even care. They didn't even try to come get me. That was when I knew I was on my own. I asked Traci's mom to take me to my bank the next day so that I could empty my account and get my money that I had worked for at my job and buy the things I left behind. I remember feeling like a Rockafeller with all that money! I stayed at Traci's for a couple weeks and during that time, I got a boyfriend, Jason. He was dorky and sweet, and thought he was tough enough to hang out with the kids my parents hated. Jason was the only one in his group with a truck, so naturally, everyone wanted to be his friend. His mom let me come stay with them after I had worn out my welcome at Traci's. It was during the time I was Jason's girlfriend that I re-met Terrell. He could tell I was vulnerable, and unsure and used that to his advantage.

He was strangely attractive to me, I don't know why but he was free and daring and that was what I needed. We jumped off bridges together and broke into the power plant to be alone and talk, we became friends. I was incredibly bored with Jason but had nowhere to go. Terrell told me if I would be his girl, I could live at his house. So, that's what I did, I broke up with Jason and moved into Terrell's house. I moved in there with minimal things, my whole life was literally in a bag, a grocery bag. We slept in the same room and bed and it was weird for me. Slowly, he broke my walls down and got in. He made me care for him and in that, I wanted to give him my only sacred thing I had, my virginity. Even if it had been taken many years prior, it was and always would be mine to give. He took honor in that moment and asked me to step out of the room so he could do something. He was in there making noise for a while and then called me back in. I went in to find he had strung Christmas lights up around the whole room and had candles going and music playing. He closed the door behind me and very respectfully kissed me slowly and tenderly. Terrell made me feel like I could have a normal life again, with him. He hit play on the CD and it was R. Kelly's 12 play and I was impressed he had my favorite CD playing. Ironically, I lose my virginity to the music of a child predator. We had sex there in that room with Christmas lights on a dimmer and R.Kelly playing.

The next morning I woke up, I felt completely different. I remembered the episode of 90210 where Brenda lost her virginity to Dylan and she looked in the mirror thinking she looked different, that was me right in that moment. I ran to the bathroom and gazed at myself. Wondering if others would be able to see how different I was now. I was a woman, and then I felt awful. I felt sick to my stomach and had an instant stomach ache. What on earth was going on? I had convinced myself that having sex had made me unpure or something and god was now punishing me. I tried to eat and I couldn't. Then, I thought, maybe I am pregnant. Oh my gosh, that's it, I am pregnant; I have to go to the doctor right now. But, when you don't live with your parents anymore and have no access to insurance, what do you do? I talked to friends who told me to go to the free clinic. I didn't tell Terrell anything, I didn't want to be without a place to live again so I kept quiet until I knew. The sweet nurse there told me I was silly, I couldn't feel pregnant from just having sex the night before, but if I truly thought I was, come back in two weeks and they would do a test to show me I wasn't.

Two weeks later, I went to that same free clinic, saw that same nurse and had a pregnancy test done. They did urine and blood, the urine was negative but the blood would be back the next day. All I heard was negative. I went home and had sex with Terrell, drank a forty and smoked a fat blunt. The next day, same thing. I had just been handed the blunt to light when the phone rang and it was the free clinic telling me I was actually pregnant. I could not believe it. I had a Newport behind my ear, a blunt in my hand and a forty on the floor all waiting on me. The woman that called asked me to come back and have a counseling session to discuss my options. I hung up, stunned, stoned and scared.

Now what? I was pregnant at seventeen and super high and a tiny bit drunk. I remembered at that moment this project I did in middle school about fetal alcohol syndrome and the effects on an unborn baby from alcohol and I was certain I had just given my baby a shitty start. Terrell came home with his mom. I was shaking and so scared, but I told him in the driveway. I had my stuff packed and was ready to be kicked out when he heard me. But, he surprised me with his reaction. He was happy, he was actually happy. His mom was too. We all hugged in the front yard and he asked me to marry him. Of course, I said yes, it was a moment we were having.

I went to the free clinic and the nurse there counseled Terrell and I on our options. He was adamant that I not have an abortion, and this woman ever so delicately said to him, "it is not your choice baby." I told her I would not have an abortion either, I didn't want one. It felt like I was cheating by doing that and I was not a cheater. Terrell and I made this baby, we would care for it. I also didn't want my child wandering around the world wondering why her mother could carry her in her belly and then give her away. I didn't want my baby to feel the emptiness and unworthiness I felt daily. They set me up with the medicaid women and got me a gynecologist appointment at the clinic for prenatal care. I was so scared. I wanted someone that had my best interests at heart and no one cared about me, they just cared about the baby I was carrying. I am out on my way back home, Terrell and I went our separate ways after the appointment, and at a gas station, and I see what I cannot believe when I pull up.

This sweet Jeep Wrangler sitting there at the pump and out gets this Jamaican god. He was strong and handsome from behind I could tell; and when he turned around, he was my friend. I knew him and I couldn't believe it. It was Darren, the only person that was sent to me that day to ease my fears. I got out of the car and ran into his arms; he was always the absolute best hugger. He picked me up and swung me around and squeezed me tight. The child inside of me felt safe and protected; but, I always did with him. He told me that Dwayne was there too, I hadn't seen him in forever. He pushed the gas station door open and it was like time stood still. I was back on the fields at Suniland and Dwayne was walking towards me, orange uniform on and helmet in tow, but I was in Darren's arms still. Then Dwayne hugged me and told me how beautiful I was in that Dwayne way he did things, so smooth and nonchalant. We chatted for a few minutes and Darren gave me his number. I had no one's number anymore since I ran away. I couldn't believe my luck to see both Williamson boys at the same time. I held his number close to my heart and we would chat often, Darren that is. For Dwayne I was always some option, never relationship material, but he was super protective of me too; not as much as Darren though. Darren and I talked almost every day, I told him about my fears and Terrell and life.

At this point, Terrell was not being very nice to me and I was unhappy. A few weeks later, it happened, I was about 2 and a half months pregnant. The thing that would change everything I knew in this house, and in my relationship.

Terrell and I got into a fight about Darren, he came home and I was talking to him on the phone. I told Darren I would call him back and tried to get up and walk out of the room. In one foul swoop, he grabbed me by my neck, turned me around and threw me into the wall; squeezing my neck and glaring into my eyes; I was paralyzed with fear. He held me there, choking me and yelling in my face about talking to another man on the phone in his house. He let go only to back hand me in a way that I thought my face would explode, it hurt so much. He walked out of the room as calmly as he had walked in. I sat in the corner crying, quietly, praying he wouldn't come back. I knew I should get up and leave, I knew I should go, but I couldn't move. It was like my feet were cemented to the floor. Fear washed over me and I was numb and I was stuck. I wiped my face and went to the bathroom to make sure I was presentable. I had a busted lip and marks all over my neck. But now it was me that was more concerned with the baby than myself. I got on the bus and went to the free clinic the next day and made sure my baby was ok.

There was still a heartbeat so the baby was good. They scheduled me for an ultrasound and said that I could only do it on certain days because the techs were all students and that was their intern day. So, in a couple weeks I will see my baby on an ultrasound. I was so excited and had something to look forward to. I got back home after the exam and Terrell wasn't home. I cleaned up and cooked for his brothers and went to do homework in our room. He came in like a bull and thrashed around and was talking so fast he could barely keep up with his own thoughts. He was higher than a kite and I had never seen him that way. He begged me to forgive him for hitting me, he said if I didn't he would jump off the roof. I didn't even have a moment to breathe before he was taking off all his clothes and running outside onto the roof. He was pacing back and forth up there spouting the most ridiculous things and thoroughly making no sense. I called the police because he wouldn't come down. They tried to get him down with no luck. He said he would jump if they came up. He kept repeating over and over that he couldn't come down until I forgave him. So, I did, for him, for my child's father. He came down shortly after I yelled my forgiveness at him and the police had the firemen check him out and told me to put him to bed and keep an eye on him. To this day, I know they should have taken him to the hospital or something, he was a child, high and attempting to kill himself. But that is what happens in that neighborhood, in that particular part of Miami that police don't like to patrol or enter; Richmond Heights.

Things got better immediately, I talked to Darren less and less and tried to make things good with Terrell. I went to school, my TRUST counselor, Mrs. Tassler, picked me up every day; she even gave me lunch money. She made sure I got to school so I wouldn't flunk and I had to just do my work. She came into my life at a time when I needed someone in my corner that only had my interest at heart. She guided me through the loss of my mother and helped me try and heal from my brother's abuse and now she is helping me again. She would drive out of her way to make sure that I got to school. She was my guardian angel disguised as this pint-sized school counselor. To this day, I hope that she always knows just how instrumental she was in my life and how her genuine care for me and my best interest helped me in ways I cannot put into words. She was my angel. God brought her to me when I was lost, and trying desperately to find my way. She helped guide me through some painful times and helped me try and heal with nothing in return for herself.

Terrell would find some way to pick me up from school most days. I think it was to see who I was talking to. This one particular day, I was talking to my guy best friend at the time, Bobby. He knew Terrell and hated him. He was being my friend and trying to get me out of my situation, and Terrell saw. He was livid and possibly jealous. He grabbed me by the arm and dragged me to the car. The whole way home, he yelled at me and once we crossed the threshold of the house, he kicked me straight in my back and I fell to the floor. He drug me into our bedroom and slapped me around. He held me down and raped me. It was hard, mean, filled with hatred and intent in his eyes. While he was doing it, he put hickies all over my face and neck. Big purple and blue ones. He was so proud of what he had done. He had raped, beat and demeaned me all in one afternoon. The trifecta was complete, I was nothing now. Any self esteem I had, went out the door the minute I was kicked through it. I even think we passed each other entering the room with that swift kick.

Bobby called me that night to make sure I was ok, and I lied and said I was. He didn't believe me and asked where Terrell was. I didn't know, but I knew he wasn't home. He could never stay home after he beat me, he always left right after. Well, Bobby showed up at Terrell's to check on me. He was not happy with what he had seen and I honestly think he was going to kidnap me if I would let him. I don't know if he called Darren, or ran into Darren and Dwayne or how it happened, but they beat his ass at the park. Or at least he told me it was them. So, in turn, he beat my ass; again. A punch for every punch he got is what he told me. The admirable men that cared and loved me, now tried to help me, and unknowingly set me up to be hurt worse than I had ever been. Before this, Terrell was a slap beater, now he was full on punching and kicking and throwing me like I was a baby doll. Pure rage when he would look at me.

After this beating, I called Darren for help, I couldn't take anymore. I needed to see what the world could be like without being afraid I would die. This couldn't have been the life that I was destined to have after escaping my step monster, could it? Darren came to get me faster than I hung up the phone. He helped me in the Jeep and strapped my seatbelt in and took me away. He was always so kind to me and in this moment he was tender and caring and very worried; he was the closest I had ever been to having a Knight in Shining Armor. He brought me to his house, where his sweet mother that had seen me grow up over the years tended to my scrapes and bruises. When Darren brought me home, he ran in with me and told her to fix me. She kicked him out of the room and told him to let her handle it. She cleaned me up and didn't judge. I looked awful and Darren only had kind words for me. I can only imagine how difficult that must've been for him. To see me, someone he cared deeply for beat that way, I will never truly know. We have talked about it over the years, but we have never really re-lived it; I don't think either of us are ready to or really need to. I am also not sure that I am strong enough to hear how hard it was for him, Bobby either for that matter.

His mom fed me wonderful Jamaican food and told me that no woman should live with bruises. That was so profound how kind she was to me. It has stayed with me throughout my life, her pure kindness to me and my unborn baby. Darren told me I could stay there with them, right at that moment Dwayne came in. He saw the cleaned up version of me and was pissed. He punched the wall and Darren grabbed him to calm him down. Darren and Dwayne took me into their bedroom and sat me down to talk to me seriously about staying there. Their older sister was in and out and she knew my sister and they offered me to stay there. I told them I couldn't. I knew Terrell would be looking for me and I had to go home. Darren told me he couldn't make me stay, but he didn't support it. He reluctantly took me back to Terrell, he told me, "I hope I am not at your funeral the next time I see you." That was hard to hear and stuck with me over the years. I knew that Terrell would kill me if I stayed there and so did he; but he did what I asked him to do.

The day for the ultrasound has come. I am twenty weeks pregnant and incredibly nervous. They call my name from the waiting room and I get up to walk back. Part of me is scared, the other part anxious to see my baby. Terrell was certain it was a boy and I didn't care what it was, but secretly thought it was a girl and hoped for a girl. I knew if it was a boy I would be dead because I would never leave my baby behind and I know I could never leave Terrell because he wouldn't let me with a son, but a girl, I could leave with a girl. The ultrasound student squeezed the cold jelly on my tiny belly, to this point I was still wearing my normal clothes and just looked like I ate two dozen tacos (that one's for you Annette). My baby is healthy from what they can see and he can't see if it is a boy or girl. He says it will just be a surprise then. Surprise! I cannot wait for a surprise, I need to be able to go now. The man doesn't understand my tears and sends me on my way.

I show Terrell the photo and he is giddy with happiness. He starts talking to the baby, rubbing and singing to my stomach. I think to myself that maybe now that he sees that there is his child in there, he will be gentle with me and not hit me anymore. That night, he sang to my belly and put headphones on it. He sang Let me Clear My Throat to my belly and the baby just kicked and flipped. I looked around the bedroom, it was no longer this room I had fond memories in with Christmas lights and candles where I became a woman, it was a dungeon filled with blind rage, bruises and memories of beatings and rape. The lights were gone, most of my clothes were gone. He took all my makeup and hair products. I wasn't even allowed shampoo and conditioner or even lip balm. Nothing that smelled nice and would attract a man. I had to use dollar store bar soap to wash my body and hair. His house was disgusting and a far cry from five bedrooms and a pool and sheets for that matter. Now my life involves dodging roaches and dog feces with no running water because his mom would spend all her money on anything but household bills and sleeping with no sheets or blankets. She grocery shopped once a month when her food stamps came in. Terrell used to take me over to his grandfather's place to eat because he cooked for the neighborhood and sold plates. That was the only home cooked food I would get other than when I went to friends' houses and his version of taking care of me. I never thought I would live this way, but I was and had nowhere else to go. My friend Jessica would have me over a lot and her mom would make me all my favorite Cuban foods, man could she cook! Jess and I would hang out in her room and her mom would come in and blow dry Jess' hair straight and I would watch in awe. It was so neat to watch their mother daughter moments, but it always made me jealous that I didn't have that anymore.

His mom got us evicted from that deplorable home and she had somewhere for her and his younger brothers to go, but nowhere for us to go. She found a cousin in the neighborhood that would take us both on and let us live there. So, off we went. I was trying to figure out how I could get out of that house, and away from Terrell when I bumped into Darren again. My guardian angel. His hugs were like safety, magic and warmth all in one. He had this ability to make me feel so protected, loved and understood all in one. He begged me to leave and come with him and I knew I couldn't. I told him it wasn't so bad because Terrell was fucking someone else now, so he left me alone. He didn't speak to me anymore and would let me starve all day and bring me food when he came home for the night. At this point, I started my Senior year and was getting bigger and hungry all the time. Terrell didn't care like he had before about whatever I did, so I would go to friends' houses every day after school and hang out. I was free, finally.

Darren stayed constant and would pick me up sometimes and feed me too. I really liked to eat!

The house we were staying in was so much cleaner and his mom's cousin was kind to me. Darren and I talked every day and would hang up right when Terrell came in; we were getting so close again and I started to look at him differently for a moment. I knew that I could never pursue him though, because of Dwayne, but it was nice to dream about how it would be. I knew in my heart Darren would never look at me as anything more than the little kid that ran around the football fields in her cheerleading uniform pining after his brother. One day, I didn't hear Terrell come in and he heard me laughing on the phone and grabbed it to see who it was. I don't know what was said between the two of them, but he hung up and he threw me from twin bed to twin bed in that room like a cartoon character; beating me worse than I ever had been beaten to date. What I saw in his eyes that day was so terrifying and hateful that it has stayed with me until this day. He beat me with the actual phone across my back and neck and told me he would cut our baby out of me if I ever thought of leaving him. This beating was bad, I was hurting, I was scared. The cousin came home and saw me and told him there would be none of that in her house, so he said "fuck that bitch she don't need to be here." He left and was so cold to me, I could only assume that this would be my chance to leave. I had a chance to go and didn't take it because I held onto what he told me; it rang in my ears, but I had nowhere to go. I had worn out my welcome at numerous friends' houses and staying with Darren sounded like an ideal situation but I knew I would ruin that welcome eventually too; and I couldn't lose Darren to that. He didn't want me there and I could have finally left, but I was a coward, paralyzed by fear and stayed. I hated myself so much at that moment and I was honestly nervous and scared for Darren. Terrell had left so angry and I didn't know what he was going to do or what he had planned. I know now, he never went to Darren, but at that moment I was sure he was. I began to clean up the room that had been destroyed by my body and his anger. I cried silently and prayed hard that somehow I would be able to live through this and leave. I called Darren's house when I was sure Terrell was gone long enough and there was no answer, I was sure he was hurt or killed by Terrell's hands. I hung up in shock and went to be alone in the shower. I stepped in barely holding my tears back and slid down the wall, uncontrollably and quietly sobbing in the shower, fearing that someone I held so dear and treasured was no longer around. I would never hear his laugh or his deep voice and the way he said my name, that was so intoxicating. I was certain Darren was gone and I would never see him again.

Later that evening, that baby he wanted to cut out, decided it was done being in my stomach. His cousin called 911 and he told me to fuck off and he thought I was faking it to get his attention. I was in so much pain. The paramedics and firemen came in the door, I remember feeling like I was safe, finally. They examined me and then loaded me into the ambulance and I heard them all whispering about me while looking at my swollen shut eye, busted lip, scrapes and bruises; and most importantly, my pregnant belly. I said "my uncle, he is a State Trooper. Call him, please, he will help me."

I don't think that they ever called. They called the police, but not my uncle. The police met me in the ER and they asked a lot of questions. Terrell told them I was running and fell, even though my injuries were not consistent with a fall any idiot could see that. I had been in that same ER four other times during my pregnancy and relationship with Terrell, and the doctors and nurses knew my name and face and bruises all too well. They also knew I was being abused, but I would never give them anything, so they could do nothing. This time was more serious, there was danger to my baby. I was in early labor at barely seven months pregnant. They transferred me to Jackson Memorial Hospital, shit this was serious this time. I remember lying in the ambulance and thinking I was going to die and my baby was too. They were sending me to the trauma hospital, the same hospital my mom took her last breaths in. I was sure that this was it for me. All I could think was, I need Darren, where is Darren, please God let him be ok and my baby.

I got there and time went super slow, but everyone moved incredibly fast. I knew no one, they assumed I had been in some sort of gang fight because I wouldn't tell them what happened. They gave me a shot, I remember it was in my ass, to help develop the baby's lungs because I was in what they called hard labor and this was my little one's best shot for life. I was terrified and completely alone. My water was leaking and they told me I was going for an ultrasound, Terrell's mom showed up shortly before the ultrasound. She looked at me, and kissed my forehead and asked about the baby, not me. At that moment, I realized that no one cared about me. The focus of everyone was my baby and not what I had just endured or me in general. In that room with Terrell's mom, the tech asked me if I wanted to know the sex of my baby. I was barely able to get it out fast enough and screamed yes. He looked at me and said the words that I knew would change my life. "You see right there, it looks like a hamburger, that is the bun and the meat and the bun. That means, it's a girl!" I was elated! This baby girl was strong and she had persevered through a lot already. I had to be strong and protect her and I was sure I would be able to leave now.

We went back to the ER and I was bound with knowledge and strength, a new found strength that came the moment he said it's a girl. Terrell walked in and I remember thinking why is he here, he hates me. He bent down and tried to be sweet and kiss my cheek, so I thought, but instead he bit down into my ear and said as intimidatingly as possible, "if you tell anyone I will kill you and the baby." I was frozen, my mouth was not going to open. He had made me terrified all over again, my new found strength was short lived and deflated as quickly as it inflated. Just as he finished his threat, the sweetest nurse came in. I had never seen her, but her name was Mercy and she said no more visitors. She knew, she was sent to help me, and I knew too. As Terrell was walking out, I casually mentioned that the baby was a girl, he looked at me and said, "I don't make girls." That was it, that was how I was going to leave for sure. I felt confident in that.

Mercy and I stayed together for a few moments and tears ran down my face. She sat on the bed and held my hand in silence. No judgment, no questions, just pure regard for me and what I was going through.

She left me there as quietly as she entered the room. I was now alone, finally and I had never felt more protected in my life. God was in that room. He sent Mercy to me in that room. He saved me from any further beating and pain. He saved my baby girl from being born too early. He protected me. He protected us. I don't know if I knew it then, but I know it now; unequivocally so. I was finally able to revel in the news that I was carrying a little lady. I rubbed my belly and told her I was going to get her somewhere safe and she would never be alone. She kicked and I cradled my belly and closed my eyes, finally fearless, safe and able to sleep.

For a couple weeks, I lay in that hospital bed healing wounds given to me from hands that were supposed to love me. A few of those days, I was inverted, trying whatever they could to keep my baby girl in. I would talk to her every moment I could. I talked to her about fears and hopes for her future. I talked to her about my parents and my life and told her it would probably be just us, but I would guard her with my life, she seemed to always be listening because she would kick when I talked to her. One day, after not having any visitors almost the whole time I had been there, a nurse gently persuaded me to call family and tell them where I was; and she delicately left a phone book on my bedside table. I hesitantly picked up the phone dialed home, what I thought was home, what had always been home; my dad.

My dad answered and I told him I was in Jackson Memorial and Terrell had beat me so bad that I almost died and lost my baby. My dad stayed quiet, I suppose taking in all that he heard or maybe mustering all of his bottled up courage. After a long silent pause, he said, "you made your bed, now you have to lie in it" and hung up. It was like I was just punched in the gut and almost instantly, tears slowly flowed down my cheek. This pain was worse than anything Terrell had done and far more damaging. I had never felt so alone or so unwanted even through all the bullshit I had endured, this was what truly alone felt like. I would have taken the beatings all over again to never feel the way I did when I heard my own father turn his back on me. Why is that ok? This was my hero. This was the man that fell in love with me as a sick infant and *chose* me to be his daughter. This was the man that adopted me and was supposed to love me unconditionally for the rest of my life. For years and years, I have wondered about this exact thing. This moment was so defining in my childhood, because let's face it, I was still a child, just a child having a baby. I was alone and my hero was gone. He had dropped his cape, closed the secret tunnel doors and flew off into the sunset leaving behind me. To be honest, he left the day he walked out on his marriage with my mom, shit he left years before that; the moment he began his affair with Sandy. I just was too blinded by his presence, my admiration and affection towards him to see that he was no longer my dad for many years now. I was foolishly hoping what we had shared through my whole life was enough to get him to help me; how naive I was.

Having struck out with my father, I licked my wounds, wiped my tears and I thought, I will just try my grandparents and see. These were my mom's parents and extremely Catholic in their morals, so I wasn't super hopeful. My Nana answered as sweetly as she was and I cried as soon as she picked up the phone. Everything that I had held in with the painful call with my dad, because I wasn't giving him the satisfaction of crying, came running out. Everything flowed out of me and through the phone, and she listened to me and I heard her love through the phone. My Nana said she would call my Uncles and someone would come, but she would call me back. My Nana was the single most amazing woman in my life. She had battled breast cancer and loved adopted babies as if they were her own. She was a true matriarch and a softy at the same time. She was remarkable and I was lucky and blessed she was in my corner. The next day, I waited for which of my mom's brothers she was sending to come and help me.

I staggered to the restroom, IV pole in hand and tried to make myself presentable; quite difficult when you're covered in yellow healing bruises. On my way out of the bathroom, I was backing out of the room with my pole and heard a gasp. Fearful to turn around and see where it came from, I hesitated, but courage and curiosity allowed me to. I saw what to this day was the sweetest most overwhelming site I have seen; my Aunt and Uncle and cousin standing there. My Nana had truly sent them to help me. My Aunt Mindy helped me back in bed and then the explanations and outpouring of support and love came. The look in their eyes when I told them all that had gone on was telling and painful to be on the receiving end of. My Aunt told me we would figure it out, but I was not going back. It was the WE part that made me feel like I was finally safe and secure and my baby would be too.

They didn't stay very long, but their visit was welcomed and gave me something to look forward to; a plan for the future. Later that night, my aunt called me and said that all of my cousins and them discussed it and they would like for me to come stay with them for as long as I wanted; my baby and I wouldn't be alone after all. Mindy told me that she was doing just as my mom would have done for one of her children. It was at that moment, on the phone with my Aunt, in my hospital room, that I finally exhaled.

Chapter Eleven

The Next Phases

*A*few days later, I was ready to go home, but my family

was not ready to take me yet. My trepidation about leaving with Terrell was overwhelming. I wanted to cling to the hospital bed where I was warm, fed and safe. I thought that going anywhere with Terrell would mean that I would never be able to leave. His mom picked me up and took me to a hotel where she and her younger boys were staying. We got food and I went to sleep. I woke up the next morning and she had left me in that room with those two boys alone to babysit them all day while she went to work. I was so angry that she didn't even ask me, she just left, she always left me to watch them without asking and it made me so mad. I was terrified that she told Terrell where we were staying and it wasn't this great hotel room; it was a crappy motel.

I called my Aunt and she and my Uncle made the trip down to come get me. I was ready to close the Terrell chapter and they were ready, I suppose, for me. My Aunt told me that I had to call his mom and tell her I was leaving and she had to come and get her boys. I didn't want to, I was so afraid she would call Terrell and tell him I was leaving. She begged me to stay and said she would protect me and I wasn't listening to that nonsense, she had already done such a phenomenal job of "protecting" me already. She got to the hotel room just as my

Aunt and Uncle were loading my "things" and I use that term lightly as I had absolutely nothing to bring except the clothes on my back. I said goodbye to his mom, she cried and I was ready to leave before he got there, and I didn't know if he was coming or not but I didn't want to wait around trying to find out. On the way up to their home in Broward, about an hour away, I remember thinking I would not blow this chance I was blessed with. I was now free from abuse and I would make the best life I could for my baby girl. I would go to college and work real hard so she could be proud of me. It was now not just me, but her, and I was ready to be her mom.

I made it there safely, and my extended family was there to welcome me. You see, my extended family doesn't do anything alone. We all get together for everything, every single thing. So, there I was in my pajamas, no bra, just as I was when I left Terrell's cousin's house that night, and a big fat pregnant belly surrounded by people that loved me and didn't judge me. I remember Grams, my Aunt's mom, walking in the house and we all sat down at the table and had one of those life talks and then she told me lets go to Walmart and get you a bra and clothes. I was so surprised that the kindness from my extended family was so genuine and my own couldn't be bothered. I was also very intrigued because I had no idea what Walmart was. We didn't have one in Miami, so this place was completely foreign to me.

We all loaded up and the ladies took me to Walmart for some bras and clothes. I didn't want to ask for anything, I took what was offered to me and was grateful. I was just honestly grateful to have a safe place and the rest seemed trivial at the time. I remember being excited to take a shower there because they had real actual shampoo and conditioner that smelled great and didn't come from the dollar store and razors! These luxuries I was unable to have in my life with Terrell brought me so much joy to see now. The only thing I asked for at Walmart was lip balm. I remember getting Soft Lips for the first time and opening the package, giddy, like a child on Christmas morning. It was this small luxury that I was so pleased to have that I drove in the car back to Mindy's and tears ran down my face while I applied it to my lips. I was not about to ask for anything else, I had my soft lips and I was satisfied. If I was greedy, I would've asked for mascara and hair products. I forgot what it was like to have clean hair and nicely full lashes, but I had what I needed and that is all that was necessary. Samantha took me the next day for a job interview at her salon she was working at and before I knew it, I had a job, new clothes, lip balm and a damn bra that fit! I was living large. I got a new OB/GYN and he was quite remarkable. I remember that he was silly and had the kindest eyes. His voice was calming and silly and stern all at the same time; real fatherly. We had to be honest with him about my predicament and what had brought me up there and he was more than sympathetic and reassuring. He took a real interest in my situation and in getting my baby girl out safely. The week after Thanksgiving, I went to the doctor for my weekly check up and he told me it was time. If I didn't have her that weekend, he would induce me on Monday pm or Tuesday am; I chose Tuesday.

Mindy and I were so excited running back to the car. It was that giddy happiness, like in the movie Annie when Daddy Warbucks decides that he wants to adopt Annie and Grace is dancing in the driveway with the driver and Punjab. I was finally going to meet this little lady that was giving me heartburn and had already made it through so much with grace and strength; she was a fighter. It was Thursday afternoon and I went home and laundered baby clothes, fixed her cradle one more time, which my grandfather made and was used by many babies in the family and I nested. Mindy and I were ready. She had taken on the role of my mom and I happily let her; I needed her and during that time in my life, I missed my mom so much. Friday night, Samantha, our friend Cami and I went and power walked the mall. Cami had us doing squats and lunges and whatever else she could think of a much different mall excursion than most teens were used to. I went home and did jumping jacks in my room, enormous and hilariously awkward jumping jacks and went to bed. I had to work in the morning. So I thought.

It was five am, and I had to pee something fierce. The whole house was awake and getting ready for work, just about, so I went to the boys bathroom to pee and headed back to my room. My bed was soaked, I was so tired I didn't care. I put a towel on it and went back to sleep until nine when Mindy called to wake me up for work. I got up and was dripping all over. I was unsure if my water had broken or not, and since I had so many false alarms, I had taken a few test strips from the last hospital stay to be sure. That sucker turned blue and it meant my water broke. I tried to find Mindy's work number and couldn't, so I star 69'ed her; 90's kids will get that one, and it was a pay phone at the restaurant she worked at.

The man that answered the phone was on his way from the men's room and just grabbed the ringing pay phone. I told him it was very important that he go find Mindy and that she was a waitress there, and he did. She came running to the phone and I told her my water broke. She screamed with happiness and told everyone she had to go that her grandbaby was being born. At that moment, I felt like she was my mom, and she cared for me. I knew if my mom was still alive, she would have been that way, so this was nice to have. I called Samantha when I hung up and told her I wouldn't be at work that day because the baby was coming. Samantha was ecstatic and said she would be right over. Before I knew it, Samantha was there and Mindy was right behind her and they loaded me up in Samantha's Purple Paseo and off we went to McDonald's, because I was not about to be starving and got to the hospital where they wouldn't let me eat.

Chapter Twelve

Baby Girl's Arrival

*I*t was 10am on December 7, 1996, the air was crisp and I had a brief moment with my belly before my life changed completely. I sat on the edge of my bed, cradled my belly in my arms and told my baby girl that I would love her as long as there was breath in my lungs and then after that I would surround her with my love as tears ran down my cheek. I was sure that I would deliver her, but I was not sure I would be able to keep her. The fears of what was to come were lingering and unkind. I was full of trepidation for what could be and what was inevitable. I knew she was coming out one way or the other, but would I have to hide with her for the rest of her life, would Terrell let us be or would I even be able to watch her grow up. All of those questions ran through my mind, the worry was real and overwhelming; so was the pain I was getting in.

The day brought through a hospital room with many family members, and new friends along with nerves. The constant was Samantha and Mindy, they never left my side for more than thirty minutes and it was to pee or eat and never together. The moments with each of them separately and together were priceless and mine and theirs and I hold onto them so tightly. My fantastic OB/GYN came in around noon, in golf clothes and I remember thinking he was such a cliche. He said I had time for him to get in a round and he would be back before I was ready to push. I thought he was cocky, how would he know when I was ready to push and how would he get back in time?

I was straight up starving and people kept coming in with food breath and I had to sit there with my IV fluids and ice chips. At some point, they gave me some "pain" medicine, but fabulous Medicaid doesn't cover epidurals, so here, have some cheap knock off that really won't take away your pain. It made me silly and sleepy and loopy all at the same time. I remember being told that I asked for my mom at some point in all this, I wondered why she wasn't there and where she was. Mindy said, "your mom died two years ago, I am so sorry." I was so loopy, but I remember crying because she was dead and I thought no one had told me. I couldn't understand why she wasn't there in that room for that important moment. It was getting dark out and I was starving and tired and poor Samantha was getting a headache. I think she had only left my side once by this point to pee and scarf some chips down. Nine o'clock came and I was fully dilated, it was time, it was baby girl time.

I began to push, as best as I could; but, I was exhausted. I pushed, Mindy and Samantha held my thighs and I screamed. I looked up from the pushing, opened my tightly shut eyes, and I instantly felt warm and secure. Standing in the background, dressed in all white, there she was, my mom; smiling at me. She was there, in that room, watching over me and watching her granddaughter be born. I knew at that moment that I could face whatever was coming for me because she was always in my corner. I knew that in this monumental life changing moment, somehow, she came to me however she could and that I would be that mom to my baby girl. The one that no matter what obstacle there was, I was always going to be there. After hearing the ugly hatred filled words from my father weeks prior, seeing my mom's ghost was just what I needed to feel like I could accomplish what I was about to do. I know and remember minimal about that day before my baby girl was born, but I know with certainty she was there, patiently watching and waiting. All the chaos of the room and nurses in and out, screaming and pushing stopped briefly while she smiled at me and mouthed, "I love you" and in came my doctor. No don't go, please don't go mommy. I pleaded with an image I saw to remain and my pain took over. I was burning now, there was such intense pain and it felt like there were fire coals on my vagina and ass. Samantha took a peak and said, "OMG she has curly hair!" I couldn't wait to see her at that point, I just wanted to be sure that she was ok.

A few pushes, curse words, a tear and lots of cries, pain and screams and there she was. This beautiful creature with ten tiny fingers and toes and curly black hair. I asked my doctor if she had all her fingers and toes and he plopped her on my belly and she gripped my finger so tight and adjusted her eyes to focus on me. She was here, she was ok and I was instantly in love. She looked into my eyes and I was no longer important, I was no longer a runaway teenager in an abusive relationship with no parents, I was her mom. They took her from me to clean her up and Mindy cried and kissed me and Samantha, my non affectionate cousin, hugged me and then told me she wanted to be a labor and delivery nurse now. I was so proud I had given her the best care I could and that I was able to push her out and she was ok; she was more than ok, she was perfect. I was infinitely more proud that I did it all without my dad and with my mom watching over me and my Aunt standing guard beside me.

Moments later, she was weighed in and given back to me. My three week early baby was a healthy seven pounds three ounces and 19 ¼ inches long! She was a vision in a pink hat, her skin was soft and delicate and her cooing sounds were intoxicating. Samantha, Mindy and I were all entranced by her, soaking up all the love she held while my torn vagina was sewn back together by my golf playing obstetrician while he told me what a great job I did. Then, in comes Terrell's mom, my heart stopped, my hands began to shake and the fear and nerves washed over me. Was he here? Was she going to try and make me go back to him? So many unknown questions flooded my brain and my breathing was erratic and I swear everyone could hear my heart beating. In that moment, I was terrified and never more grateful to my Aunt Mindy for not leaving my side and keeping her arm around me the entire time his mom was there. I think I held my breath for the entire conversation with her waiting to hear her say he was outside and coming to take her. He was not, thank you God for that moment, thank you times infinity. She told me that she thought my baby looked like her, and I disagreed, then she asked me what her name was. I hesitated, mostly because I didn't want them to know anything about her. I wanted to keep her safe and hidden from all of Terrell's family. Now you can judge me all you want, I don't give a shit, my first responsibility was to my baby girl not to anyone else. Her "father" beat me regularly while she was cooking in my belly. How was I to know he wouldn't do the same to her? I didn't, so I behaved and acted as such, because that was all I knew of him now. All the early memories of how nice and caring he was to me were thrown out like last night's garbage when he began to hit me. I told her my infectious childs name and she said she would be back tomorrow with Terrell, but not before saying that she expected that my baby girl was going to be named after her like Terrell wanted. Who gives a rat's ass about what HE wanted!

Welcome to the world Kayla Marie.

Kayla was taken to the nursery for a bath and I got moved to my new room out of Labor and Delivery. It was a spacious room with a window overlooking the night sky and dark and cold; just how I love it to sleep and I was so tired. It was in that quiet moment before she went home for the night that I asked Samantha something special and specific. We sat in my room together, both exhausted and elated from the long day, illuminated only by a TV. I looked at her and asked her if she would be Kayla's Godmother. She cried and said of course, and she was honored. What she may not have ever known was how honored I was that she accepted. She had always been that person I admired and strived to be like, and now my baby girl would have this strong woman in her life forever. I wasn't sure at this point how long of a life I would have, I was terrified daily that Terrell would find me and finally kill me. So, choosing Samantha to be her Godmother was strategic as well. I knew that if he did eventually succeed and kill me, that she would fight for my baby girl until her last breath. This amazing person never left my side, except to pee, and she would always be there for Kayla the way she had been there for me; I just knew it.

Slowly everyone left my room and it was just me alone in my new motherhood and full of nerves. My night nurse was so kind, she could tell I was scared and uneasy with what being a mom was all about. She sat with me, rubbed my hand in hers and talked to me about just making sure I was there for my child, that was how children knew that they were loved at the end of the day. I was in a sea of emotions and didn't know if I would ever stop crying. I laid there in that dark cold room illuminated by moonlight and the glare from the TV, my own thoughts and fears were getting somewhat drowned out by some infomercial on TV and I had this instant and overwhelming need to see my baby. My mind started to panic and thought what if Terrell's mom was lying and he had come there and taken her from the nursery?

I ran from my room, down the hall to what I thought would be the nursery and it was but the blinds were closed. My nurse saw me out of bed, and scolded me playfully. I was shaking and there must have been fear in my eyes, because she told me my baby was getting her first bath but as soon as she was finished, she would bring her to me. I didn't believe her and begged her to show me. My heart was beating so fast and I was convinced that she was gone and I had only had a brief moment with her. I thought that this must've been what my birth mother felt like when she gave me up, or at least I have always hoped she did. How would my precious gift know I was her mama if she was taken from me? I think that she could tell that I needed to see her now to ease my racing mind and before her "no" response was out, she said sweetly, hang on. She went into the nursery and opened the blinds, there was another nurse in the back washing my Kayla. She held her up for me briefly and Kayla looked so at peace. Pink and content with the warm water on her skin and looking so serene and simply gorgeous. I began to cry again, and my nurse came back and hugged me tight. She told me I did good and I could relax while I was here, that they would protect her. I actually believed her. It was then that I knew that I could breathe a little, but not fully. I knew that she was safe and I was too. She pulled back, smiled at me, wiped both our tears and took me into the nurses station for some food. She let me have whatever I wanted from the fridge. I thought I hit the motherload, this was where all the jello and pudding was!

She took me back to my room and tucked me into my bed and told me to eat. She was what I needed that night and in that moment. I needed a mother and she mothered the hell outta me ever so gently. Reluctantly, I inhaled that jello and pudding with a turkey sandwich. Then I heard a knock on the door and my nurse was back, this time with my baby girl. She turned her towards me, fists in her mouth and smelling like pure delight and rainbows; she was finally in my arms, for good; this was what heaven must feel like. My baby girl was breathtakingly beautiful, this perfect little creature that God chose to be mine had surpassed all the violence and came into the world in pure perfection and bliss. She didn't have the easiest beginning and one that I thought would seriously hurt her, but now, the future looked bright for her and I would make sure of it. I talked and she cooed and stared at me while I memorized every inch of her face. I cried and she pooped. I smiled and she breathed. I stared and she stared. I sang and she listened so intently. It was the best first date of my entire life. Nothing compared to that peaceful moment, late at night in the dark room of a hospital, in the maternity ward of Northwest Medical Center, the day I became a mom.

My amazing nurse came back to take my Kayla back to the nursery so I could sleep some and I passed out rather quickly. I was still in some pain from childbirth, but it was nothing I couldn't handle. The next morning, I was blessed with the arrival of my grandparents. They made the drive all the way from Hialeah to Margate, which is about an hour and they were elderly, so this was an honor. My Nana walked in eager to see the latest addition to the family and my Papa staggered behind carrying Kayla's infant carrier. They drove all the way up to surprise me with it, I was so grateful to them for that. My mom couldn't be there for this but she sent her mom and dad and it was amazing that they came all that way for us. We got to spend some time together and talk about how mom was in the room with me at the time I was pushing, my Nana's eyes filled up with tears and maybe joy that I was able to have her there still. The nurse brought in the lady of the hour and my Papa was the first to hold her. He told her that day that he would always be her Papa and always love her. He held her the way that he had held all of his grandchildren, like a sack of potatoes. Then it was Nana's turn and I could see the pure joy in both their eyes while they held Kayla; they were proud and happy and I was honored to have given them that.

Shortly after they left, Terrell and his mother were supposed to arrive and Mindy made sure I was not alone for that. Mindy was holding Kayla and when they came in, she handed her to me. In that moment, my stomach dropped and I was sure he would hurt me right there for disobeying him. He didn't, he took one look at his daughter and softened his expression. He came with his mom and uncle, who is scary in his own right. I mean this man picked someone up, flipped them around and slammed them on their head when he was a teenager! Scary is not even the right word to describe him, it is more horrifying. Terrell wanted to hold Kayla and I let him, I knew something he didn't know. The hospital had an ankle bracelet on Kayla that if she was taken close to an elevator or stairwell, would shut the whole place down, so he could never leave with her; that was whispered to me the night before by my kind night nurse. I felt powerful and armed with knowledge he didn't have, so hold her all you want, she isn't going anywhere.

The time unfortunately came for me to fill out the birth certificate, something I did not want to do with him there, and something I continued to put off all morning trying to make sure Terrell was nowhere around when I did it. You see, he had demanded Kayla be named after his mother and given his last name; I was not doing that. I had named her and that was what I decided and she would have the same last name as I did. I avoided the papers as long as I could before he realized what I was doing. I filled them out, looked at Mindy holding Kayla, I knew she was safe, and walked out of the room towards the front nurses station; trusting Kayla with Mindy. Terrell followed me, and yanked the forms from the nurse to see; mind you he couldn't read so I was not sure what he was doing. He did, however, know what his mother's name was and his last name, so he didn't see that anywhere on the page and became enraged. He demanded someone tell him what his daughter's name was, and I looked at him, armed with my newly found courage and said, "Her name is Kayla Marie." He took off running towards the room and stopped at the door. I pushed myself in and took Kayla from Mindy and took off towards the nursery. I don't know what happened behind me, all I knew was the nursery was locked up and he wouldn't get her in there. I couldn't run, but I tried with every ounce of strength left in me, and I got there. I banged on the door and begged to be let in. The nurses ushered me in quickly and they called the police. He was screaming he would take her from me and I wouldn't leave there with her. I was terrified and instantly knew I needed to protect her with everything I was and stand up to him once and for all, for my Kayla. The police came and Mindy was in the nursery guarding me like a top notch center when his mom asked to come talk to me. I reluctantly let her in and Mindy did not leave my side. She pleaded with me to let her be a part of Kayla's life and I told her I would think about it. But, I looked up at her, Kayla tightly secured in my arms and asked her, "why should I let you see the child that he almost killed and you did nothing to stop him from doing it?" She had no answer, turned and walked out peacefully, not before calling my Aunt a "string bean." The police escorted him into my room and he cried at my feet begging me to forgive him, I ignored him while he latched onto my legs begging, and the officers told him it was time to go, I was numb to him at this point. He kissed Kayla and then me, unwelcomed, but he did it anyway. He turned around at the door, looked back and said, " I love you bae." The officers advised them that they were not to come back to the hospital again and issued them all a trespass warning. I exhaled as tears ran down my face and Mindy stood at the door making sure they left.

Dr. Mark Scheinberg, my amazing OB/GYN, came into my room shortly after all this went down, he had been briefed by the nursing staff, and the police hadn't left yet. I was still sitting on the edge of my hospital bed holding Kayla so tightly and emotionally broken with tears running slowly down my face. It was like a scene from a movie. I felt so many emotions at that point. I was scared he would be waiting for us in the parking lot. I was proud of myself for standing up to him and standing my ground. I was sad that Kayla's first hours were filled with not only happiness but terror. He entered and comforted me instantly. He tried to remove Kayla from my arms and I resisted at first and then I let her go when he reassured me she was going in the crib next to me. My arms were shaking from holding her so tight and for so long. I watched him closely and carefully put my priceless gift down and sank into my tears. He grabbed me and hugged me like a father does. He wiped away my tears and told me my first and only responsibility at the end of the day was to the beautiful baby girl he successfully delivered early. He looked over at Kayla and took her from the crib. He held her up and told her she had a good mommy and kissed her on the forehead. He sat with me and said to me, you did your part and I did mine, let's send you home so you can heal from all that happened over the last twenty-four hours. He had told me the night before that I would be there for a few days because of my tear being so bad, so being there less than a full day was plenty for me. I was ready to go home. He had arranged to have me taken out of the kitchen where they get semi truck deliveries so that if Terrell was watching, he couldn't follow us. Samantha was called to come help in this, and Mindy was there too. The amazing nursing staff scoured the hospital floor and grabbed all the baby supplies they could for me. I was beyond touched to see how many things they donated to me and my baby girl.

They loaded up the cart with all the diapers, wipes, bottles, a diaper bag and a baby's first time capsule. I was ushered into the wheelchair,

Kayla in my lap in her new carrier and surrounded by nurses; they cocooned us. It reminded me of how my friends would help me pass through the halls of High School while pregnant so no one would bump into me. Mindy reluctantly left my side to get to her car, but left me in capable hands. She loaded up her car with more baby supplies than I think anyone ever got leaving the hospital and Samantha and I headed to the staff elevator to take my new baby girl home for the first time, accompanied by security and my nurse. This was not the movie bringing the baby out of the hospital and heading home that I had envisioned, but it worked. The elevator landed on the bottom floor and we were greeted by security officers that helped get my beautiful daughter and I in the car. We pulled up at home and the whole house was decorated for Christmas, decorated for Kayla's homecoming. My uncle had really outdone himself. There were lighted arches and Santa with his reindeer on the roof. When I got out of the car with Kayla and walked under the arches, I stopped for her to take it all in and she was mesmerized. This little person that so many people awaited and protected, was now safely home and wrapped in love with the whole sky lit up just for her to walk under.

A month later, he attempted to break into my house. He was halfway in my cousin's window screaming for me and Kayla in the middle of the night. I was terrified and so was my cousin. We called the police and they came out and examined the area around the house and the window he tried to come in through. They found fingerprints and footprints in the sand pile that was outside her window. That was enough for a judge to grant me a restraining order and one for Kayla too. He tried to claim in the courtroom that I was the abuser and the judge laughed at him.

That same month, it was January 1997, Samantha and I went to Miami arena with some friends of ours to the New Edition Reunion Tour. He knew I was going and showed up there. He stood outside the arena looking for me and by some chance, I saw him before he saw me. Our friend Drick, who was with us, threw me over his shoulder and Samantha gave me her jacket to cover my head and he ran me to the car. While he was doing that, Samantha talked to some police officers and let them know what was going on. We pulled up the arena to pick up Samantha and my heart was racing, he was still walking around determined to find me. Samantha got in and said that the police were going to give us an escort to the Miami Dade County line and we were safe, I was safe. I stayed crouched down in the back and then would pop my head up every few minutes to be sure no one was following us. I was so terrified, but grateful for the City of Miami police officers that escorted us back.

The next few years, we lived in that home and all of Kayla's milestones were done there. We were part of a family and together we enjoyed it. But, I got restless and wanted to actually be Kayla's mom, not take a back seat to Mindy. It was so incredibly hard in a home with a personality like hers to be Kayla's mom. She stepped in and did things for me and I watched, reluctantly, because she knew better. I just wanted the chance to be Kayla's mom and make all the decisions. I justified it by telling myself that I am a child raising a child, what did I know. She had raised three kids already and seemed much more skilled at it than I was, so I let it happen; until I didn't want to anymore. I turned twenty one and found this new need to be a better mom and person. I had been very flippant with my body and relationships, never really letting anyone in long enough to love me the way I knew I deserved because love to me was disappointment and pain. I kept some friends at a distance and lovers even further away, but I wanted my Kayla close.

Chapter Thirteen

The Beginning of The Rest of Our Lives

*M*y girlfriend Mandy that I had met a few months

after Kayla was born was moving into this great apartment by the beach in Fort Lauderdale and there was a two bedroom apartment coming up for rent at the end of February. The woman that ran the apartments was so kind, she let me do my deposit weekly until I moved in and I couldn't wait to have my own place for just Kayla and I, and to be close by the beach. The only thing left to do was tell Mindy and that seemed to me to be the hardest part. I never wanted to let her down and some part of me felt that I was, even though she knew we wouldn't live there forever. I think I hurt her by telling her I was moving out, I don't think I let her down, I may never really know how she felt. I think she was proud that she had gotten me to the point where I had a GED now and a good job, so moving out was inevitable. I still hated that I hurt her and the guilt was a lot to bear. I hated that she was angry with me and that was the last thing I ever wanted. Mindy had become the mom I was missing quickly and lovingly; I depended on her so much for her maternal approval. She was the person I wanted to impress more than anyone else and the opinion I cared the most about. I had absolutely nothing to move into this place, but I was moving out nonetheless.

I found a great deal on a new bedroom set for me and Mandy let me use a bed she had in storage for Kayla to sleep on and her couches for my living room. Mandy helped us move into our new home and she was a couple doors down. Kayla loved it because she could run over to Mandy's and she loved running back and forth through the second floor. Our building was very Melroseque, a two story building with a courtyard in the center with a picnic table and the pool adjacent. It was small, but it was our place and we loved it. What I didn't get from Mandy, I purchased from GoodWill or yard sales; this was living on my own. I had no clue how to cook, or do laundry Mindy had done all that for me. Mandy showed me how to be an adult and do all that and I can never repay her for all she did for me. I quickly mastered Shake n Bake chicken and parmesan noodles, which was Kayla's favorite. We were so close to the beach, which in turn meant we were super close to bars and clubs.

We met a neighbor two doors down from me and she had a little girl too. We arranged to swap weekends watching the kids so we could each go out on the weekends. It was like this single parenthood shared custody agreement. Mandy, Michelle, Nicole and I would go to Baja's, which was this super great 90's club, almost every weekend. We pregamed it at Bootleggers, our favorite bar on the Fort Lauderdale intercoastal where Mandy was seeing the bartender. We drank for free there, mostly because we were girls, but also because we were hot. We just tipped out the bartender and we were on our way! It was our own personal Cheers, where everyone knew us and if they didn't they did shortly because we were so much fun they'd want to be around us. We never met anyone that didn't like us or wanted to hang out with us.

Those were the days, carefree, young and full of life. Dancing and hanging with a group of ladies that genuinely loved each other was remarkable, those were some of the best memories and times of my life. Some have gone separate ways and some remain close, but we all stay in touch.

Mandy met the man that she would marry in that apartment complex, just one floor down. Her future husband was this massively muscular man with a sweet genuine smile. He quickly was annoyed with us mostly because we were obnoxious girls because we could have fun anywhere and all the time; but that almost as quickly adored us. We all became instant friends and it was evident that he and Mandy had a chemistry that was undeniable. Kayla adored this man and lovingly called him Pizza Man, because he came and brought us a pizza one night and she thought he was the delivery guy. He would scoop her up in his massive arms and she looked so small, safe and loved. He was always our protector and always there for us all.

That time in my life was also during my fireman obsession. Ah, the sweet, sweet love of those handsome men. I still don't remember how it happened, the fireman obsession, just the theatrical version in my head. I was working as a cashier at Publix and the Fire Truck pulled up. Most of us know they come to the grocery store to get food for their days when they are on shift. I didn't pay it any mind and kept working. Suddenly, the doors opened and it was like fog machines and sexy music began to play while these men entered. One of them smiled at me so intoxicatingly that I could have melted in his dimples right there, I was drunk on those dimples; I wanted to live in those dimples. I tried to maintain my composure, but failed horribly and quite awkwardly when that same sexy dimple faced fireman entered my line. He was kind and charming and sexy as hell and wouldn't stop flashing those dimples. Just then behind him another one equally as sexy with dark and soulful eyes entered with a quick and shy smile, not a big confident one like the other guy. They both chatted with me and each other, but it seemed that dimples had his eye on me and I did not mind one single bit. The next couple of days I began to notice that I was paying more attention to when they came in, looking for dimples, I didn't know his name yet and his friend, the strong silent one.

A week later, in walks the two of them, again cue the fog and music. I was most likely drooling, because they were not in their normal uniforms, they must've just done a training exercise or something because they had on shorts and t-shirts and smiles. Here comes dimples with his items in my line and he chatted me up and then asked me if he could take me to dinner because he couldn't stop thinking about me. SAY WHAT! Little ol' me? What! Obviously, this was the cheesiest line, but nineteen year old me ate that shit up with a fork *and* spoon and licked the remnants on the plate. Of course I played coy and told him I would think about it and he handed me his number, his name was Dan. I was so excited to know his name, finally. A few moments later, the other hottie entered and just chatted me up and he also gave me his number, but he was different. Less suave than Dan, but equally as exhilarating. He was Levi.

Dan and I immediately started talking and getting to know each other, Levi was a little more laid back and hesitant. He and I became friends, instantly. I seemed to know that he was going to be a friend, but I liked him. He was strong, sexy and sweet. He had this heavy Puerto Rican accent that was such an eye opening turn on that some days it was hard to even pay attention to what he was saying. Dan was more direct in his wants and desires. He was thoroughly attracted to my younger self and had no issue letting anyone know. Levi had a thing for a co-worker and while I set that up, Dan and I explored what we had between us. We went out on a "date", it was far from it. I knew what I was getting myself into with him. I knew what he wanted from me and what he didn't. Dan was older and extremely successful in his field, but I felt special with him. We went to his house and that night he showed me what sex was supposed to be like. He showed me what an orgasm was and what it was like to have multiple ones at once. I was instantly hooked and forever changed. He was this skilled lover, that was confident in his skill, but was not relationship material. It was a shame, because no one ever made me feel the way he did. I felt sexy, capable and desired with every touch he gave me. He would stare at me in this seductive way that made my panties wet and made me want to have him take me wherever we were. It was that look of, I've seen you naked and I'm planning the next things I want to do with you; that dirty look. Dan showed me what it was to be a woman and be desired and devoured by a man. I had no idea that sex could be so connected and amazing. He always made me feel incredible in the way he did things. He would look at me like he couldn't wait one more second to devour me and then kiss my body while he ran his fingers slowly all over me; yes it was as hot as it sounds! I was disappointed when it ended and so was my orgasm.

So, Levi is dating this girl I worked with that was very pretty, but she was unsure of him and that pissed me off. He was fantastic, what was there to be unsure about? At this point Levi and I were very close and great friends so I knew a lot about their relationship, hearing it from both sides. I of course, in a jealous fit, ruined his chances with her. I don't remember how, but he seemed to care minimally and laughed it off in front of me. Levi was this intricate creature, scared to love and even more afraid of commitment, so naturally I had to try and change that. I would show up at the station when he worked, Dan and him were on different shifts by this point and bring him food or flirt with him. He finally caved, and kissed me one night behind that station in my car and I never felt anything like that kiss. My whole body was a part of that kiss and before I knew it, Levi was the one smiling at me when he came into the grocery store and making an effort to see me after his classes. I was on cloud nine. Levi was the personification of what I wanted in a man. Strong, silent and sexy, but so good to me. He was a good man and with him, it wasn't always about me being naked, like it was with Dan. He wanted to know me and put in the effort. We spent a lot of time sitting and talking together getting to know each other. Levi was so intriguing to me, my mission was to break his walls down and have him fall in love with me.

Levi had me at his house and we had not had sex by this point yet, so I knew it was coming. I nervously drove all the way to Miami where he lived, and got to his house overcome by nerves. I walked up to his door and he wasn't there. He had told me that he may be at the pool when I came, so I should head there if he didn't answer. He was at the pool, singing, smiling and glistening in the water with a beer looking every bit like the cover of a Rolling Stones magazine. He hopped out, turned down his classic rock and I admired the water slowly sliding down his chiseled abs; he wrapped his arm around my waist in one smooth movement, kissed me and took me upstairs to change. This was the first time we would spend all day together, so Levi suggested we swim before dinner. I changed into my bathing suit, and we went back downstairs. Once I dropped my towel, he stared, hard like he had never stared at me before. I liked it a lot! I was super hot then, hello twenty year old body where you at girl!

We cuddled in the pool, kissing each other. I gazed at him singing and playing air guitar in the pool, my gosh it was intoxicatingly sexy! The sun was starting to set and Mike thought we should head up to get changed for dinner. We got out of the water, Levi wrapped his arms around me with my towel and dried me off. We got upstairs, I was still incredibly nervous and he told me I could shower first. I took off for the shower and Levi stayed in his closet looking for something to wear. I reveled in the idea of being in his shower and seeing all the products that make him smell the way he smelled. I remember feeling sexy and trying to be that way in the shower, in case he came in. I watched General Hospital, I knew what men did when women showered. I was able to shower and get dressed without Levi entering the room at all, sadly; he was such a gentleman. I walked out of the bathroom, Levi was jamming out to music again and went to shower. While he was in there, I changed my dress three times. Levi came out and took one look at me, smiled and said, "we match." I didn't get it at first, but we did. We were both wearing blue and white. Him a blue and white guayabera and me a blue and white babydoll dress. We went to leave and get into his truck, he was nervous and fumbling his keys; it was adorable and I felt amazing that I made him nervous at all; because I could have crawled right out of my skin I was so nervous. We get in and he is taking me somewhere that he won't tell me, which drives me insane, but he needs to make a pit stop at the ATM first he tells me. Well, if you have never driven in Miami, with a nervous guy, don't. He was apologetic with every curse word and finger, he ran over the curb at the bank and we finally made it to this amazing spanish restaurant he couldn't wait to take me to. I couldn't get over that he was nervous because of me and that was endearing to me.

The meal was excellent, the company impeccable and we made our way back to Levi's. In the truck I got closer to him to cuddle on the way home and he wrapped his arm around me. I had been in this truck before, many times, but this time felt different to me. We got back to his place and he parked. He looked at me, leaned in and slid his hand up the side of my face and kissed me. It was like no other kiss we shared or I had shared before. This kiss was passionate, romantic and full of meaning and feeling. Levi had never kissed me so passionately and intensely before. He got out of the car, walked around and reached his hand out for me to help me out of his truck and into his arms. He walked the entire way from the car to his condo with me in his arms. Yes, it was as hot as it sounds! He was a fireman for goodness sake, he better have hot moves like that one! Whew, hang on getting a little nostalgic here!

Anyway, he fumbled with his keys and kicked the door open and dropped me on the bed every so slowly while staring into my eyes. Since that night I have longed for a man to be able to recreate that feeling and no one has; some have come close, but not quite the same. We made romantic, passionate, mind altering love that night. It seemed that whatever I had been doing sexually prior to Dan and Levi were like juvenile basics compared to these men. These men showed me what it was like to be desired and for me, after all I had been through, I never thought that was possible. I never thought sex would ever be anything enjoyable or somethign I craved, until that moment.

Chapter Fourteen

39 Forever, yes please!

$\mathcal{I}$ have over the years, jokingly called this time with Levi

and Dan my sexual awakening. But it is nothing compared to the awakening I got at 39. It was like I woke up one day and I was a horny teenage boy, like all the time with an insatiable desire that couldn't quite be scratched. It has been the strangest and most incredible thing all at the same time to live through. I feel sexier, I feel more sexual, I feel the need for sex often.

So, shortly before I turned 39, I stumbled into exercise; kickboxing to be exact. Somewhere in there, with my incredibly attractive and fit trainers smiling at me I became confident again. In that I started to try and forget the man that just destroyed me and caused me to sob uncontrollably for weeks in my walk in closet. I exercised every day, ate right and felt super powerful; I was punching and kicking away the hurt I felt. I would walk into that gym and see my incredibly sexy former MMA fighter turned trainer and my dear friend who was the other trainer and I had to not only be sexy again, but feel it too. Tony and Henry inspired me to push harder each time and motivated me to come back to class, every class every day. I wanted to be proud of myself again and that included my body. Plus, how would I ever get him to date me if I was an overweight mom?

I mean, realistically, I knew he would never date me, but it was fun to pretend and it honestly helped with the motivation. It was nice to be flirted with when my heart was so damaged. It was nice to feel someone look at you again and notice the curves you had always been trying to hide. There is no hiding when you are a sweaty mess kicking shit. I thank my friend Henry every day for telling me about that gym and for giving me Tony and him day after day. They brought it with every class and I only hoped to remotely measure up. Walking into that gym daily, I made friends, got my waist back and found my confidence again. It was quite possibly exactly what I needed and exactly at the right time. I think that having a minimal crush on Tony was what made me better. I realized soon after the crush started that we were in two completely different places in life and that he would never be interested in me; so I changed my view of him.. He has this weird innate way of pulling the truth out of me and getting me to say things that I don't want to talk about. I can't bullshit my way out of anything with Tony and I think that is what makes me value our friendship and him as a person. He is real, and honest about who he is always. He convinced me on that first day that we met that he could help me and he was right. He helped me more than I think he will ever know or understand. He gave me my life back. Under the different colored lights and in between the sweat, thai and tear drop bags, he helped me become me. For that and for always making me own up to my own shit, I am eternally grateful.

I also felt like it was time to date again and that's where I came across Brian. Brian was this super attractive and very fit guy who works out at Gold's and he has the most beautiful blue eyes. Samantha and I renamed him blue eyes so when we talked about him, my child never knew who he was, plus I loved calling him that and giving him a nickname. Brian was fresh out of a marriage that destroyed him and I was out of a relationship that destroyed me too, so we were perfect; for a night or two. I had the best first date with him I had had in a very long time. He made me feel what I was trying to get back, sexy and desired; wanted. Then, he pulled the rug out from under me and took it all back, and I felt like shit again. I liked him though and this was hard for me to accept. He seemed to be able to handle my bullshit and my need to joke around and it didn't scare him; so I didn't let him push me away. I called him up after what was quite possibly the worst date I ever had, where the guy dined and ditched me with the bill at Bonefish! You know who you are, you piece of trash. Whoops, off topic.

Anyhow, Brian was appalled for me and I invited him over to hang out and make me feel better. I knew what I was doing, I was horny and wanted someone that found me sexy after being humiliated; Brian knew too without me telling him, and he found me sexy. He ended up at my house shortly after I got home from the awful date and I changed into my jammies and he laid on my bed while I took off that night's amazing makeup job; what a waste of foundation it was. Somehow, after hanging out in my room, being my most authentic self, which I can be around him, we started to kiss. That he found me sexy, in sweats and no makeup was electrifying to me. From there, I won't give you all the sorted details, but we had sex twice and it was the shit you write poems about and gaze into stars and shit; but kinda heavy on the porn too, it was hot! Blue eyes made me feel like I had been missing out on great sex my entire life. He made me feel sexy, desired and devoured. Brian got a high five from me, because it was just that impressive. We've had sex a few times since and hung out since. He showed me sexual positions that I never ever knew existed and made me question what kind of sex I had been having over the years. We enjoy each other's company, but Brian is fearful letting someone in will destroy him again, so he stays closed off. But he's a great friend and ego boost and we share a love of chicken wings, beer, football and sex.

I seem to only find unavailable men in my adult life. When I was in high school, I was liked, but it seemed simpler than adult life. Apparently, you actually have to leave the house to meet someone decent, who knew? Then like my life, the trainwreck reappears, my married "ex". I use the term "ex" very delicately, because we were in fact nothing romantic for him at all during our time together. I was completely enamored by him. He reminded me of my father, this tall, dark, and handsome man at my first real corporate job. He was intelligent, poised, observant, reserved and intoxicating. He smelled like those boys we all wanted to smell like in high school, so much so that we stole hoodies and other attire to have their scent on us. That was Jason. We met shortly after I started my new big girl, my, I got a degree in Business job, and we began to talk. At first, it was simple, friendly and playful, then before I realized it, we were talking all day all the time about ourselves. You know those talks, the get to know you talks, all single women crave; it was like that. We spent hours talking and gazing at each other in a very taboo way so no one knew. I would get in my car to leave and my phone would ring almost simultaneously with my door closing. He was always a gentleman with me and I ate it up like warm chocolate cake. He didn't realize how hard I was falling until we decided to have an actual evening date together. He came up to my house after work, which was quite a haul from Charlotte; he reminded me how much he hated sitting in traffic and I reminded him how important I was. It was sweet and dreamy and a bit condescending all at the same time. We sat and talked, drank wine and flirted. He grabbed me and kissed me passionately and with purpose and directed me towards my bedroom. This was it, we were going to have sex!

He pushed me back into the wall, slid his tongue down my neck and kissed me while lifting my leg up against his body. He stood there, one arm holding my leg the other my ass and I was lust drunk in the moment; it was incredibly hot!

We went into my room, where he slowly undressed me kissing every inch of my body that he removed an article of clothing from. He lifted me up and laid me on the bed and began to devour me. He went to slide his penis in and looked into my eyes and then stopped and stood up. WHAT! What just happened? He looked at me and said, "I needed to see if I could say no to you."

Yeah, go ahead and pick your jaw up, because that was how I felt in that moment, defeated and shocked all while lying there naked and exposed. I immediately hopped up and started to get dressed, he grabbed me and tried to kiss me. I wasn't having it, I was so embarrassed and ashamed and I just wanted him gone. He left with a kiss on the cheek and I grabbed the bottle of wine and retreated to my bed to drown my sorrows. I bawled my eyes out and drank the entire bottle; I hated how he made me feel at that moment. The next day at work, he told me he wanted to talk to me. He knew I was falling and he couldn't reciprocate, so he ended it, in a very analytical, very Jason way. He analyzes every single move, decision and outcome, why would I be any different? I instantly hated him in a theatrical way, just so he knew. But, when he looked at me, time continued to stand still. No one was there, it was just us looking at each other. It felt safe and warm. He was my own personal blend of heroin dressed in business casual. He confessed to me that he was in a relationship and he couldn't be in both, so he chose the one he was in when we met. I was broken. I had to ride the stupid elevator back upstairs with him and he kept asking me if I was ok. I looked at him as the doors were going to open and said, "no I am not ok and leave me alone." I meant it too. I wanted to be anywhere but there and anywhere but in his eyesight. He didn't intend on me falling for him for that matter, so this was just not in his playbook.

Like most addicts, we go back to what broke us, and why would a 6ft tall handsome man be any different? Jason and I worked together when he got married, though he never told me, until he got back from his honeymoon and I saw this band on his finger; that was like a knife to my heart. This man went off, told me he was going on vacation, but got married! Who does that? I don't think that he actually *could* tell me what was going on. I think that it was painful to him to know he was torn between two women, one he was marrying and committing to, and one he couldn't have. He left shortly after and I thought, oh good, he is gone I can move on now. Wrong! Just like herpes, he reappears when I don't want him to and when it is convenient for him and when my life is calm. He pops up once or twice a year, when I assume his marriage is boring him and he tries to be in my life. I used to tell myself, we are just friends, it is ok. But he would always find a way to make me smile and look at him differently than just a friend. Up until recently, I have been able to not give into him and not be with him. This time was different. He spoke all the right things and told me he was separated and it was like before I knew what was happening, my vagina took over and my panties were off. Mouths were active and hands in places you can't do in public without getting arrested. He touched my body the way it needed to be touched, the way it desired to be touched; the way he should have years before. He made love to me the way it had been achingly waiting for. We spent many nights together, much more than we had ever up to this point. We laughed and had sleepovers, was this actually happening? I was so shocked. He wanted to meet friends and would call me on FaceTime when he had his kids and couldn't see me; he even brought them to my house once. This was what dating him was like and it was better than I had thought. He was kind and attentive to me. He stared at me that same way still and it always made me feel slightly uncomfortable and highly addicted. I was so blindly happy and didn't realize that it was all so incredibly one sided. Then, the reality of him and his ways set in and when I pushed back, he did too, except I wanted to see if he would fight me on it and he didn't.

You see, like most men I date, they are more important than I am in their eyes. Jason was no different. Everything involving him and regarding him was more prevalent than anything with me. At first, I thought it meant that he was just driven, then I realized it was actually because he was selfish and spoiled. He expected me to drop everything I had going on for him because he made himself available to me, and I did. When a man does this to you, the best thing you can do is pull out your mirror; AKA, your friends. Those are the people that actually hold up the reality check to your face and say, do you really hear yourself? Are you truly going to turn yourself inside out for him? Jason knew that as strong a woman I was, he was a weakness only because I wanted to be loved; bad. He knew that was what my heart needed and he sprinkled his little crumbs for me while I ran behind sucking them up as much and as quickly as I could. We have always had two different visions of our relationship. He thinks it won't work because I can't handle his life's demands and that is ok to let him think that. It's really because I don't have the energy to always be last in line for someone that is fantastic in bed, incredible actually, but emotionally unavailable.

Just as I thought that I was able to let go of Jason and what could be of a relationship with him, he shocks me and out of the blue, won't let me go. He has finally done what the little girl inside of me has always wanted, he chose me. I put my foot down and told him what I would and would not accept and he complied, happily so. It was like this enormous and pivotal moment for us. Jason has always been this unattainable man. This larger than life person that the insecure girl in me always thought I was not good enough for. The more I got to know him and his analytical, obsessive compulsive ways, I began to still feel that way. That was when I decided to push him away, completely. I cut off sex, and kissing and ended it; so I thought. Because I despise confrontation as much as I despise kale, I obviously texted this to him. His response was swift and manly and what I never expected. He called me the moment I walked out of work and told me that wouldn't work for him. He was fighting for me, this was how he showed me that. He patiently gave me a week to think things through after telling me that he wanted to pursue us and give us the fair chance we have always deserved. Then, as decisive as he has always been, he reached out and asked me for a date. He had always told me that my definition of dating was different from his, so I felt I needed to be clear in what I wanted. I accepted his dinner invitation and made it clear he was to pick me up. He agreed, with smooth confidence and told me he would be there at seven. I told him I wanted a traditional date, where he picks me up and we go out and then come home; no sex. Jason gave me that and more. From the moment I walked out of my bedroom to see him standing there, it was like a dream. I could hear him and Riley having conversations about our day at the Renaissance Festival and I nervously touched up my makeup.

I walked out and he was staring at me in that seductive Jason way he does. His eyes light up and twinkle and his smile begins to widen showing his amazing teeth and his voice gets deep. He led me out of my door with his hand strategically placed in the small of my back, after he whispered in my ear how beautiful I looked, not sexy, beautiful. We head to his car, where he starts for his door and then turns and runs around behind me to open mine. It was like that scene in Footloose when Ren picks up Ariel for the prom, he was nervous and I was too, I could feel it. He gets in and we start to drive, and he reaches to hold my hand. Are you fucking kidding me!? I have been waiting for this exact moment for three and a half years and it was finally here and I was not letting go. I had set out on this night with zero expectations, and had really tried to tell myself it would be horrible and he could never give me what I wanted. But, right there, with him holding my hand and being in the moment with him, I forgot it all. We get to where we are going, this outdoor shopping and restaurant area and he realizes he didn't make a reservation, I know we will be waiting forever for a table because it is always so busy where we were going, but decide to make the best of it; since he was beating himself up already for the lack of reservation. I suggest we walk around and enjoy the evening. This is my favorite place in North Carolina. It is so calming and serene at night and it is always all lit up. It is very romantic to walk and talk with someone you care for through the shops and hold hands. I told myself, his behavior in public will show you how he feels. We walk out of the restaurant and start heading around the shopping area and he grabs my hand again, it was warm, safe, natural and strong. We walked hand in hand, very comfortably, just taking it all in. We kissed in stores and smelled chocolate being made and enjoyed being playful with each other on our first real date. It was the best date I had ever had and it was nothing glorious or over the top. It was me and him just finally being able to be together and we soaked it up; together. I didn't know where this would go and how long it would last, but I do know that I had dreamt about it all for almost four years and it is right here. I just had to reach out and grab it and not push it away. I wonder if I am strong enough to actually get a happy ending and know that I deserve it.

Through my therapy, I have learned that PTSD is what has driven my relationship views and that there is a little girl me that is begging to be loved and chosen at the end of the day and through everything. I don't know if I have the strength to tell Jason all my history, I don't know if he wants to know. I just know that right at this moment, he is choosing me and choosing us and that feels unreal. It feels like a dream. Like I may finally get the happiness I have searched for and it happened under my nose without me paying attention.

I had completely pushed him away. I told him I was done with him and done with all the games. I didn't want to continue this relationship and he should let me go. Apparently, that didn't sit well with him, and if I am being honest, it didn't sit well with me either. Shortly after this sudden change in wants and desires with him, he goes and does what he does best. In true Jason fashion, right when I think that he is what I want, he pulls back; and then, so do I. We start barely speaking and not seeing each other and it becomes very apparent to me that he is just not my forever, he is not even my right now. He was never anything for me. He made me feel what I was lacking. Sexy, listened to and desired. Hardly the things to build a lasting relationship. So, I realized it and thankfully before I was this dumb woman in love with him, I ended it. I was able to leave this manipulative, selfish one-sided relationship intact; strong and armed with the knowledge of what I do want. Sometimes, someone else can awaken in you what you never knew was lying dormant. Something that you thought you had stuffed away in the back of your heart never to resurface again.

My love for Massimo.

Chapter Fifteen

Massimo

*W*ell, we have reached the part of the book where we discuss the man that I spent weeks crying about in my walk in, Massimo. Oh gosh, my stomach is flipping up and down like a tilt-a-whirl here! Massimo was and will forever be a great love and my deepest regret rolled into one person.

Some time in June of 2017, I started noticing his FaceBook posts again, I think I had unfollowed him at some point. Massimo and I ran in similar circles when I moved to Fort Lauderdale, he still thinks at times that we went to High School together because he feels like I have always been there; but Mass, once again, we never did. It's actually kind of cute that he thinks he has known me so long at times, and others it is annoying as hell! He shared this post about Jay-Z and Beyonce at a concert together singing what was, I believe, their finale on the tour, Forever Young. It was a beautiful display of two peoples love and relationship and very Queen B. She was decked out and looking gorgeous while Jay looked dapper in his best skully draped in all white. He commented that this was the kind of love he was looking for, or something along those lines. I watched it and instantly wanted to remind him that he could have had that if he didn't fuck it up years before. Massimo and I tried this whole let's date thing 10 years prior and it didn't work because he was a huge partier then and I was not even remotely that way. He playfully responded and it began.

Before I knew it, we spent every non working moment on the phone and some working ones too. See, Mass lives in Florida and I live in North Carolina. So, a long distance relationship was for us. Days passed, and I became attached to my phone and FaceTime. It was our own private nightly date. We had no other choice but to talk and get to know each other and that was amazing.

While talking to him on FaceTime and packing to move to a new place I learned so much about him and him about me. He sang to me sweet romantic old school R&B and heartfelt love songs. Mass is terrible at talking about his feelings, but he can pick a song to show you how he feels. One particular night I remember like it was yesterday. Him in his white robe, drinking his scotch and smoking pot, me just completely entranced by him. He told me he wanted to call my ex-husband and tell him we were together. He said he had known him his whole life, and it was the right thing to do. I was overwhelmed with feelings and in that moment, I knew I loved him. I was done. He called my ex-husband and told him, only because of their relationship in the past and because we share a daughter, Riley. Massimo knew that being with me meant being with Riley and he embraced it, but needed Michael's approval. He hung up with me and called Michael. I eagerly waited for his call back, on the edge of my seat. Would Michael be rude, talk massive amounts of shit about me or had he matured and would he accept the olive branch Mass was extending? I don't know what exactly transpired, but Mass called me back smiling that provocative smile he gave me and said Michael was cool. After he told me, he asked me to be his girlfriend, and it felt like I had waited my whole life to hear that.

After I accepted, he instantly changed his FaceBook status to in a relationship and he played me the most romantic song that going forward, would be our song, and the song that every time I hear it I am instantly taken back to that moment. The feelings in that moment, the sounds, the smile on his face, that twinkle in his eye and his voice. That song, oh the sweet beauty in that song and the words. I swear it's like it was written for us. When I am feeling particularly Massimo nostalgic, I play that song and feel like maybe, just maybe one day he will be what I saw him as. That song was Keith Sweat's 'I'll Give All My Love To You.' I implore you to listen to it, breathe it in with all it's romantic glory and read the lyrics.

Massimo, as much as his swag doesn't allow him to admit it, is a sweet man, that is romantic. I think that the Italian in him, the noisiness of him minimizes all that and he allows it. But with me, he was tender, playful and attentive. I flew down to Florida for a long weekend to see Mass for the first time in August. I was astonishingly nervous to go, but full of anticipation. I flew into Orlando and my dear friend Rachel made the huge drive to come get me, delayed flight and all; Love you Rach! I felt instantly better when I saw her. Rachel is that friend that puts your mind at ease with delicacy. We drove the three hour drive to Mass and talked the entire way about everything, except Mass and my nerves; it was just what I needed. We made the turn into his condo complex and it was late, and very dark. Ok, nerves were flowing deep now and Rachel was a calming sounding board. She told me, look if it is not what you think, you call me and I will be right back here and we will have a great weekend together. I was instantly blessed to have her as a friend and almost at ease, there was a way out. If it wasn't what I anticipated, I could always call her and I could leave and never look back. I always need to see the exit in everything and everywhere or my anxiety and claustrophobia sets in.

I couldn't find his building and called him, he told Rachel to back up and there he was. Standing there smiling in a black Hanes T-shirt and Old Navy heart pajama bottoms. Looking every bit the man I was in love with, my god was he sexy. I hopped out and into his arms, where I wanted to live. Like a gentleman, he met my friend, put her mind at ease, grabbed my bags, watched as I hugged her goodbye and slapped me on the ass to send me upstairs. YES! In the elevator, we were both in awe. We couldn't stop awkwardly smiling and touching each other, not sexually, come on people! Gosh!

We got inside and he showed me around. He was still working and asked me to sit with him at his desk. He pulled up a computer chair for me and put my legs on his lap rubbing my feet and working. I got to stare at my man, I was finally with my man. He leaned over and kissed me, for the first time and I was sold. That moment was romantic comedy worthy. It was not scripted, but felt too good to be true. That kiss, everything was in it. That Keith Sweat song, the weeks and months we spent on the phone, his desire, my desire and our love. My entire body was shaking and he noticed. I was so overwhelmed with being in his presence and just being able to actually touch him. Every conversation we had, every song he played or sung, every twinkled smile played through my head as he slipped his hand on my cheek and into my hair and kissed me. He went to try and pull my computer chair on wheels closer to him and, well, in a completely unromantic totally me way, he made me fall out of it and onto the floor. So much for being graceful, sexy and desirable. I immediately started laughing. The tension that was in the room broke and he was like, "what are you doin on the floor?" and came down to be with me. He laid on top of me kissing me and said, "you gotta be careful, we are gettin up there and could break a hip." Ass. He was older than me, and was telling me that I could break a hip. I asked him to get me up and we went to his bedroom. I put on a playlist of all the songs he had sung to me to date on the phone, and there were a lot. We kissed and began to make love, real love. He looked at me and sweetly and intently said, "I hate you". I instantly started sobbing, his dick was still inside of me and I couldn't contain my tears. He wrapped his arms underneath and around me and held me while I cried. It was his way of telling me he loved me. He has some weird thing with those three words, so instead he playfully has said over time, 'I hate you' instead. I knew what he meant. His eyes told me what he meant. His actions told me what he meant. This was it, we were in love and I couldn't have been happier.

We had a great few days together. We hung around his condo, he cooked for me and we went on walks; hand in hand. We swam together at night and he wanted to take photos of us, and wanted them to be just right. So we kept taking them over and over. He was what I imagined and hoped for and more. We walked over to his clubhouse there because he wanted me to see how great it was inside. We walked in and he told me that this was where we could get married. I was flabbergasted! He has actually thought about all this? We sat in this amazing room overlooking a lake and talked and planned and just breathed each other in. But, our picture perfect visit was coming to an end and I couldn't handle it. Unfortunately, I had to go back home and I had a full blown panic attack.

Think Christina Yang on Grey's Anatomy, season one where she starts crying after her miscarriage and can't stop, so she screams, "somebody sedate me.". Yep, that was me, except I asked him to come hold me. He did in this swift motion that wrapped me up in my future. I saw it all. Growing old in those arms, loving until my last breath and watching our children become parents; all in those arms, those glorious arms. Going home was extremely difficult, leaving him and watching him leave me, not knowing when I would see him again; but the next few days were worse. I had had a taste of what life with him would be like and I was a full blown addict, get me an IV of what he was putting out, addicted. The reality of going home and not knowing when I would see him again was overwhelming to say the least, it made me miserable. I found comfort in our talks, how we felt about each other and his eyes. He told me what he needed from me and I really tried my best to soldier through his request. He needed me to be strong and patient. To not cry when we left each other, because that was just tragic to him and too difficult to bear.

So, I tried, stumbled and consistently failed. He drove me to the bus station and held me the entire way while I cried. When we pulled up, he got out and walked me inside and we said goodbye. I was empty, it was awful leaving him. He stayed up and texted with me for the few hours it took for the bus to get me to the airport in Orlando and then he went to sleep and I boarded the plane to head back home. I told him I would fly him out for Labor Day because it had been a couple weeks since I had seen him and his birthday was shortly after, so we could celebrate. I bought his favorite cologne and that round trip ticket, then I headed out to Raleigh a couple hours away to pick him up. I could not wait to lay my eyes on him and my arms around him. He got frustrated with me because I didn't know where I was going, I had never been there and well, I am wretched with directions. I was so incredibly nervous and he had the nerve to be angry with me for not knowing how to get to an airport that I have never been to. I finally found him and he was working on his phone and barely gave me the welcome I hoped for, or deserved for that matter. I hoped he would seem excited to see me, shit I just flew him here, but work, again, was more important.

Over our relationship, I found out where my place was in line of importance to Massimo and let's just say it was not after his daughter where I should be. Coming to that realization was quite humbling and painful. We drove the next two hours almost in silence while he worked and barked orders at me. I was feeling so stupid and defeated. How could I have misread that entire situation, misread him? I turned to him while I was driving and said, "Are you done? Are you ready to be happy to be with me yet?" He looked at me and said "of course I am happy to see you silly." So, here was my opportunity to tell him he needed to show it, and I choked, I froze. I let the momentary pause between us go long enough that he started babbling about work and my feelings were shit again. I wished that he had just been able to see my feelings and how it was sitting there not being given attention by the only person you wanted it from. We got home and he immediately started working. I had imagined we would spend the day naked and in bed, but he had work on the brain instead. He noticed I was unhappy shortly after we got there and ushered me onto his lap where he cuddled with me and apologized; he essentially pacified me so that he could continue what he wanted to do, work. He was always busy and I just wanted one day where he chose me over making money. One day where I felt number one in his life and heart. One day that we could just enjoy each other, revel in our love and talk about anything and everything. We sat together at the table, working and him rubbing my feet. It was much better now, and I was happier. Riley came home from school, eager to meet Massimo in person and see if mommy was really happy. We spent the evening together as a family and spent time bonding with each other, most importantly including Riley in it all.

Massimo cared deeply for Riley, it was so completely evident with how he spoke to her and with the ease at which he showed her things. She instantly became his sidekick and his GPS to the grocery store the next morning when he wanted to make us all breakfast but didn't know where the store was. They left together while I slept and came back and started cooking breakfast together. This is quite possibly one of my most favorite Massimo memories, sitting at my kitchen table watching my two loves cook me breakfast together and dancing around with each other. It was like he was meant for us. I danced while I cooked, Riley was my sidekick and now she had a stable man in her life that resembled her favorite things in her mommy. We had a wonderful few days together. We walked in the park and had a picnic while Riley and some friends played. Bailey, our maltipoo, came with us on this park day and he and Massimo had become super close, he was a traitor to his mommy I joked. We had a great family time together and we spent that time making memories. I had won tickets to the Ed Sheeran concert a few months before for Riley and I to go, but the concert was the same weekend that Massimo was here. Riley looked at me and told me that she thought Massimo and I should go because she only knew a few songs from him and it wouldn't be fun for her. I knew she was lying because I played Ed Sheeran all the time, every album, every car ride; she knew. She was being kind, giving up her ticket so that Massimo and I could have more time together. So off we went to have a great night with meet and greet passes too!

We walked into the arena and were taken with a bunch of other people with meet and greet passes too on this weird secretive backstage journey. We waited a few minutes and then we went to meet Ed Sheeran. We posed for a photo, he joked with me because I had an Eminem CD in his CD case; when he opened it up he said, "proper." He told me that was how he worked on his stutter growing up and listening to Eminem and that was it; we were done. Massimo and I went to find our seats and wait for Ed to start. I had always loved him since his first album when Kayla introduced his music to me. His voice was impeccable and his songs were stories and lyrically fantastic. Ed started, and Massimo was mesmerized. He played every song that was perfectly Ed and Massimo was so impressed that he had no band, just him. He played 'Thinking Out Loud,' and Massimo grabbed my hand and kissed it. He was mesmerized by the song and the feelings that washed over him. When we got home that night he drew me a bath, I got in and he took our relationship to the next level, he took a dump while I was in the tub. I was disgusted and appalled but also kind of strangely happy that he felt that comfortable with me. He joined me in the tub and played 'Thinking Out Loud' while we cuddled in the tub by candlelight. I joked that it made me think about the scene in Pretty Woman when they were in the tub together. I was in heaven in my tub with him listening to Ed.

We had spent the next couple days shacked up together in romantic bliss, but again, he had to leave. But, there was a hurricane coming directly towards his home and he had to come back; I was afraid for him to be there. We got to spend so much time together over the next two weeks that he was there we really connected. I would come home from work and he would have dinner started, the house clean, the dog high and sleeping. He would get up every morning when I would get up for work, he would get up with me and make Riley breakfast and walk her to the bus stop. I was enjoying watching how involved with her he wanted to be and how attentive he was to me. We woke up together and went to bed together and it was so amazing. One day I came home from work and he was yelling on the phone with someone and I was uncomfortable because I had never seen him that angry. He started explaining the reason he was yelling and I just couldn't understand what the yelling was for. It was some issue with someone talking about him and he didn't like it, but I thought that if there was no truth to the lie why did he care?

I have never really cared what other people thought about me and I thought he was the same way, but I was really wrong. We argued about this and he didn't like that I didn't understand where he was coming from and how important his reputation was to him. We actually argued and went to separate ends of the house. He finished cooking dinner and I took a shower. I couldn't believe he was angry with me because I didn't see it the same way as him. When dinner was finished, he came into the bathroom to tell me it was ready and looked at me, put his hand under my chin, smiled and apologized. We talked it out and heard each other's points and it was our first real fight and we handled it pretty well. We lay in bed that night snuggling and talking and I asked him if he had heard of the Five Love Languages test. He hadn't and I explained that it would help him understand how to love me better and the same for me. He was excited to take it and asked me to find it for him. He was so cute taking so much care with each question to give it the thought it deserves and answer how he deeply felt. We laid together reading our results and learning about how to love each other correctly. It was almost perfect. I didn't want him to leave, I didn't want him to go anywhere. He was happy here, loved it, and he was calm. I wanted that for him, he was always so high strung and stressed, but Florida was his home and off he went.

Over the next couple months, our relationship went from being those two people discussing how to love each other cuddled up in each other's arms to two people that could barely have a discussion without one of us getting angry. Massimo has a daughter, G, and she has been held from him for a long time because her mother believes that Massimo molested her. He was very forthcoming and we talked about it at length, he had been honest with me from the very start with the situation. I believed that Massimo never touched her, and so did the police, a judge and Dr. Phil. The mother called the Dr. Phil show to thoroughly discredit and embarrass Mass while trying to strip him of his parental rights to G. I begged him not to go. I knew him pretty well at this point and he is a hot head, true Italian with his temper, and those talk shows only want ratings. He tried to convince me that the producers were telling him that they believed him and it would be in his favor when they taped; I still didn't agree. I just wanted to protect him and keep him safe and his reputation which he had told me meant so much to him. Why go? Why put yourself in the middle of the scrutiny and court of public opinion, but he needed to do this. He needed to know at the end of the day if he never saw G again, that he fought for her and he fought hard. That same reputation is also why he went, he needed to be able to walk around the rest of his life without that title hanging over his head.

So, off he goes to California with a pissed off girlfriend waiting to hear what she thinks. If you've seen this episode, which I don't know how you couldn't, it's like the highest rated one, you know he was right. I still didn't know and fought with him while he was there, and called bullshit on everything. He seemed to be looking forward to the show and the taping and I couldn't understand why and I couldn't protect him and it drove me nuts. I behaved really badly and was not nice, but nevertheless he persisted, and told me it would be ok; I wished I had his confidence. Filming day comes and I call him before they start. He answers, hyped and nervous. I tell him no matter what is said I love him and support him, but don't let them make a fool of you and we will get through this. Then he says, they are calling me to go. So, when my man walks on that stage he is scared, nervous, excited and fighting with the woman he loves. It was all evident in his face and eyes. He looked broken and in pain, and that pained me for my part in how he felt, I will forever regret my behavior. I told him I would never watch him up there once I saw the preview and saw him that way, and I stuck to it for a long time. Those same twinkling smiling eyes were sad and full of fear and anticipation. It was not what I wanted to see from those eyes. He filmed his episode, got on a plane and came home. When he got back, he was different, we were different.

We fought consistently now, almost daily, things were changing for him with court and his daughter and I seemed to no longer play an important role. It was unsettling and uncomfortable to be pushed away that way. We went from talking everyday, throughout the day, to barely once a week. I was confused, heartbroken and lost. I begged him to stop ignoring and avoiding me and he promised he would, but never did. That was the beginning of the end for Mass and I. November started and I felt so incredibly alone when it came to my relationship, I was barely holding it together and Mass was further than ever. I tried everything I could to get him to talk to me the way we did before and he just couldn't or wouldn't, I wasn't sure. Being in a long distance relationship, conversation is vital and gives the relationship the life it needs to grow. I finally got him on the phone after incessantly calling until he answered; not my finest moment. I told him he needed to just leave us alone and focus on getting his daughter back because he had been ignoring me and I wasn't happy with it and that was not a relationship or the one I signed up for. He was pissed, it came from nowhere in his mind and it was all I had been thinking about for a few weeks.

He feels like I turned my back on him when he needed me the most and I saw it as I was walking away from the love of my life for his daughter. I sacrificed our relationship so that he could focus on fighting for the one relationship that meant the world to him, the one with his daughter. He showed me almost overnight how sad he had become after coming back from Dr. Phil and I knew that I was only an obligation to him at that point and not someone he loved. I couldn't be that to anyone and I couldn't allow him to feel like he had to be in a relationship he didn't have the time, energy or focus for. It will forever be a regret that will linger with me. In trying to help him in the only way I could and thought was best, I destroyed any chance of us being, an us again. He didn't fight me to stay and I wanted him to. I didn't fight to stay either, at first. I've reached out to him, he's reached out to me. It's this back and forth dance that we know the music to and yet we can't figure the steps out. Distance plays a role, but his hurt and anger plays a larger role. The day he is able to let it all go and love me the way I am and understand completely why I did what I did, is the day that this can stop being a back and forth dance of missteps and missed opportunities. I am just not sure that I will see that in my lifetime. Mass is in love with Mass, and I am not so sure there is room for me in there too. So many things were left unsaid and unresolved, which is why a year later we are still doing this dance. Why neither of us can simply say 'fuck it' and walk away for good. He irritates the shit out of me and I love every second of it and he knows it.

I did finally watch that episode of Dr. Phil, but only and I mean only because he asked me to. I texted him through it and cried alone in my living room watching him cry. I had only seen that once and that time, it was because something touched him not because he could finally breathe. That other time I saw him cry was a profound moment in our relationship. It was shortly after he asked if I would be his girlfriend and talked with my ex-husband, that it happened. He had shared so many beautiful songs with me about his feelings, without speaking them, and it was my turn. I was falling in love with him, almost instantly from that first phone call, and I wanted him to know how I felt and feel safe in my love. My favorite artist is Christina Perri, she is this remarkable song writer with a powerhouse voice that gives you all the feels. I asked Mass to listen to one of my favorite songs by her, 'The Words', and he did; while we were on FaceTime. The song begins with beautiful piano beats and then her soft voice sends chills up your spine.

I watched as the man I was falling in love with listened to it intently and felt the love in the song and her voice. The line in the song that made him cry was in the chorus. He heard and felt it and I watched his eyes swell up with tears, and he took a deep breath. He sat back in his chair a little more and relaxed, listening, allowing the tears and music to fill him up. Then, almost purposeful, she belted out the line that made him smile and stare at me with that sexy twinkle in his eye he had whenever he looked at me lovingly, "Still your mind, now I'm yours to choose." That was it, he got it. In this moment, this man was my man, and I was his woman and he understood what I was trying to convey through someone else's words. At this point in our relationship, he was going through so much with his ex and feeling the loss of time with his daughter. I would like to think that the tears were all for me, but I think that some belonged to G. This case and this battle had consumed his life and ripped his daughter out of it. He was broken when we found our way to each other and I like to believe I helped in rebuilding him and giving him love.

Hearing that Dr. Phil believed him and the audience applauding was powerful and overwhelming to him that he broke, finally and let out his pain. I broke too. Watching him up there all alone, with no one there in his corner and the woman he loves being a total bitch to him. I was selfish and regretted how I treated him. I thought fighting him against going was protecting him and it wasn't, it was protecting me from the shame of molestation, the shame I wore everyday. I had not really told Mass about my past very much, I gave him little morsels, but never the whole cookie; very few really knew, until now. This topic is painful to me and unbearable, and I didn't want the man, the person I loved more than any other man, associated with a word that caused me so much trauma. He never knew why, he never got to; it just seemed like I didn't support him. When in reality, I supported him so much I couldn't bear to watch. I made it through the whole two-part episode and was changed. I looked at him differently. I looked at him as a stronger man than I saw before and one that had endured a similar pain that I lived through, and he lived through it too.

He finally got his daughter back and the smile on his face is bigger now than when he smiles at me. Maybe that was why I was in his life, to teach him to smile again so his daughter could see a happy daddy. Maybe it was to teach him how to love again since he had been so closed off for decades. The questions and the maybes drive me nuts when I try to figure them out, so I stopped trying. The distance has and will always be a large hurdle between us, but there is so much more that can be easily solved with action and effort. That is all I need. For now, I hold onto his memory and the love we shared and wonder if this is just a semicolon in our relationship or an actual period. Hoping that one day, those same songs, drenched in our love and memories, won't hold as much power as they do now. I hope someday, maybe, I can let go of all this and move on.

Chapter Sixteen

Marriage and Michael

$\mathcal{T}$o explain the true gift of love that motherhood for the

second time is, I have to go back to my marriage to Michael. He wasn't a bad guy in any way when we met, he was and is just a spoiled, selfish man and we were much better as friends than husband and wife. I know that may seem rude, but it is not meant that way. Michael and I made that peace a long time ago and we try to co-parent Riley everyday together. Some days are much easier than others, but the attempt is genuine.

It was January 2005, and Kayla was wrapping up her soccer season, and for those of you who can do math, it was shortly after my attempted suicide. We were on the soccer fields and my cousin Jamie was talking to Michael. Now, I had seen him weekly on the fields, but never spoke to him. And if I am being honest, I was never attracted to him, ever. Jamie knew him and they chatted while I watched my handsome nephew play soccer, my mister; my most favorite boy. Jamie came back over to us and said Michael asked about me and wanted my number. After immediately saying no and not being in a place mentally where I should date, Jamie spent the rest of the night trying to convince me to date him. It worked eventually, and I called him up and we went for ice cream that night. He came to pick me up in his annoyingly loud, but fun to drive Subaru Impreza with a blow off valve dressed like shit in blue basketball shorts and his keys around his neck. I thought, gosh I hit the lottery with this slob. But, he was kind and funny and the fact that I wasn't attracted to him went away because he made me laugh and feel safe. He was sweet and had my best intentions at heart always, in our beginnings. We instantly spent every single day together and after a few weeks, every night. I fell in love with the idea of Michael, but he deserved me to love him wholeheartedly and I just wasn't able to. I was happy and knew I could be happy with him if I tried. He asked me to marry him, in front of my entire family, on Mother's Day a few months later. This should have been a red flag of enormous proportion because he did not know me at all. He proposed to me in front of so many people with a ring that was not even remotely my style.

Now, the ladies will understand this. A man that loves and is in love with you, knows what you like and what you are afraid of or uncomfortable with and has only intentions of making you happy. This man did not know me at all. I hate big crowds, they actually make me highly nervous and I like a lot of diamonds, he got me a solitaire. We planned our wedding and he was extremely involved, nauseatingly so. We got married in March of 2006 and our problems started shortly after. We had three bliss-filled months of happiness, and then it was like a light switch turned off and he was unhappy and miserable all the time. We fought constantly and had just attempted to get pregnant on the Fourth of July, hoping it would fix our marriage. Friends of ours got married on July 8th and I knew I was pregnant that day, so much so that I didn't drink at their wedding. I went to my doctor at the end of the month and she confirmed it. I was pregnant. After miscarriages and an abortion, I never thought this would happen. In fact I was told it would be impossible.

I went to the doctor on a Friday for a blood test and on Saturday, all hell broke loose and we could never come back from what was to come. We got into an argument, and honestly, I have no clue what it was about. We screamed and yelled and Michael does not handle adversity or fighting well, he retreats and belittles. So, as he was packing his bags to vacate our three month marriage, I was unpacking everything he put in and Kayla was on the bed in front of both of us. I don't quite remember what exactly started this, but I remember him calling me a "Fat Bitch" and it was like he punched me in the gut. I was sure I was pregnant and I was not fat. How could my husband, the man that swore to love me in good times and bad speak to me that way. Besides, he was no prize and definitely not thin, so who was he calling Fat? He spit in my face and I went to slap him and he grabbed my wrist and pushed me back. Once you have put any hands on someone out of anger and not love, the relationship is done. He slapped me instead and I punched him repeatedly in the arm. He grabbed my shoulder and pushed me down, while Kayla hit him with the cordless phone over the head. It all happened so fast and then he was gone. I was left there with Kayla scared, completely shocked at what had just happened and sure I was pregnant. I hated him for doing this to me, he knew what Terrell did and promised he would never lay a hand on me; he lied.

Monday evening, Kayla had a basketball game and Michael was there because he worked there. We briefly spoke and I told him that we need to go to counseling and you don't just walk out on a marriage. Just then, my phone rang and it was my doctor, personally calling me after hours to tell me I was in fact pregnant. I was elated! I never thought I would carry another baby. I looked at Michael and we hugged and he ran around the parking lot screaming, "I'm gonna be a dad!" We mended our issues and put them aside to enjoy this pregnancy together. The weekend prior, he had told me I was "a fat bitch" and left our marriage for the safety of his parents' home, what a difference a few days made. But there in my belly was a miracle.

I went to my gynecologist and had my first pregnancy visit, with lab work and a pap smear. A couple days later, I got a call from my gynecologist saying I had to come back because I had some abnormal cells in my pap smear. I had just had my annual pap that year and thought it was an error. It was not. I had some abnormal cells that if they didn't do some procedures on it would turn into cancer during my pregnancy. So, into stirrups I went to have my cervix scraped and try to get the cells out. It was painful, but I held onto her telling me that I would have to do it one more time and then I was done. We went home and tried to move on with the pregnancy. Then the 16 week visit with all that blood work came around, and again, I got a call. This time, my midwife, Christine Johnson (she is absolutely the best and was seen on ABC news for a parking lot delivery) called me directly to break the news to me. She said, "I don't know how to say this to you, but your baby came back with a high chance for Down Syndrome - 1:300." I was speechless; I am crying writing this.

We spent over an hour on the phone together, mostly crying, but she was there for me answering any questions I had and just crying with me. She knew how much this pregnancy meant to me, what I had already endured with the abnormal cells and colposcopies and she empathized with my pain. Through the tears, fear and uncertainty, we discussed my options and she referred me to a perinatologist, because abortion was not an option for me. Michael had other fears. He thought about the strain on us and the financial aspect more than the child. I had never felt so distant from him. He wanted me to abort and I refused. I knew whatever God had decided for this baby, I could handle, even if he couldn't. Heck, I had already been a single mom once, I was certain I could do it again.

I went in and had a 3-D ultrasound done. In this they look for characteristics of Down Syndrome, specifically a nuchal fold. My baby did not have that. The ultrasound tech asked if I wanted to know the sex and I said "of course."

Michael was sure that our baby was a boy, and I was certain it was a girl. A few seconds later of me lying on an exam bed with my belly exposed full of cold jelly and Michael on the edge of his seat the tech says, "It's a GIRL!" I was overjoyed. God had blessed me with another baby girl, Michael sat quietly, pouting. We went in to see the perinatologist who said the only definitive proof was an amniocentesis and I wanted definitive proof because as she explained to me it would have been better for her delivery to have the right people in the room to help her immediately if needed. So, the amnio was done and we waited on pins and needles for ten days until that phone call came, no down syndrome. I don't think I ever felt relief like that in my life. My pregnancy and my marriage continued to be a nightmare until the end. It was truly a condition. I suffered from gestational diabetes and preterm labor along with vaginal scrapes and down syndrome scares, I was done being pregnant. All while doing it alongside a man that was pulling away from our marriage and unhappy within himself.

I couldn't figure out why he was pulling away from our marriage and our family. Michael had semi embraced being a step father to Kayla but not fully. He did what I asked him to do and it helped take some strain off me. October of that year was another major turning point in our relationship. It was the day of his nephew's birthday. His friends had come for the party, and his family and us ended up back at his parents house after the party ended, to hangout. We were all sitting on the porch and picking at Michael as we always did, but something I said hit a nerve and I have never been one to back down, so he had given me the shut up eyes and then told me to. I was angry he embarrassed me in front of his friends and mom and he was acting like a child. I was like whatever Michael you are such a baby, and he walked over and kicked the chair I was sitting in so hard that I came off it a little. His friend, who is a police officer, scolded him and reminded him that I was pregnant, it seemed he had forgotten. He was like "fuck her" and stormed off. I was mortified and cried in the bathroom. Now everyone knew what our marriage was and I couldn't shield it any longer and I didn't want to. Gestational diabetes was difficult for me to handle and I didn't have his support to make it any easier to navigate. Before I knew it, the early term labor came along with the diabetes and now I was on two different medications to keep me stable. A month before I gave birth, I was put on bed rest and he was extremely unhappy. Now the sole financial strain was on him and he couldn't deal. We made the same amount of money and honestly, I never understood while I was in it how he maintained our household on just his income. After 4 more amnio's at the end to assess her lung development and some false labor scares, she was ready to come and I was anxious for her arrival. It seemed like we had waited so long, but she was still coming earlier than expected.

On March 21, 2007, I got a call from the perinatologist telling me her lungs were ready to be delivered and they had me scheduled for induction that evening. I laid in Michael's parents bed watching American Idol with his mom and eating my last meal before meeting my baby girl, an Oreo Blizzard from Baskin Robbins. We went to the hospital at 10pm that night and began the induction at midnight. It was uncomfortable to say the least. I had to lay flat and not get up for 12 hours! All while having a catheter in me and listening to my husband snore. I was nervous, uncomfortable and also still not convinced my baby was ok; coupled with being in the same hospital I had delivered Kayla in and endured the end of Terrell's abuse, made for a very lonely night. The next morning the nurse told me that the doctor would be back around noon to remove the Cervadil and begin the pitocin part. So, in came the doctor to remove what felt like sandpaper inside me and just then a big gush. I was so embarrassed, I asked her if I just peed on her and she told me no I that my water broke. It was real now, she was actually coming!

Chapter Seventeen

Baby Girl #2

$\mathcal{E}$arly in the evening on March 22 my beautiful baby girl

made her arrival. I had endured an overnight induction and the most painful delivery to see this gorgeous creature. The epidural went in around 1pm and shortly after, they had lost her heartbeat. I was terrified, but they had a plan to regain it; an internal monitor on her head. Well, that is about as fun as it sounds. They put this monitor on her head to keep track of her and have to keep checking it frequently because it kept falling off. I was so uncomfortable. With Kayla, I never had an epidural and all my friends swore it was a life saver, but not for me. I was still in so much pain, when the nurse told me that the epidural works by gravity and I should roll on my side. I did and it seemed to take a little pressure off. I was lying on my right side and in comes a whole slew of people, they had lost her heartbeat again. I was so scared that something was wrong with her and wanted a c-section just so that they could get her out quickly. I still wasn't convinced that she didn't have Down's and honestly, I held my breath on that one for a long time after she was born. At some point around 5 o'clock, I asked Michael to come rub my back because the pain was intense. He removed my sheet and said the bed was full of blood. Michael ran out of the room to grab someone and my eager baby girl was crowning. Here they all came running in again, the Doctor, I was to be her last delivery in the USA because she was going back to London, and a midwife, not my Christine, but Jessica and she was equally as skilled. I made a ton of noise and Jessica looked at me and said "no noise, put all that into the push."

Two pushes and out she came looking like what I can only imagine heaven looks like. This was a familiar feeling and moment, it was one I had shared so many years prior and was gifted with again. She was plopped on my lap and it was as if we were all alone. Every ounce of noise in the room was gone as I gazed upon this elegant person. Everything and everyone was gone in that moment, except her and I in sweet maternal bliss; I was in love. I wanted to inspect her and keep my eyes closed all at the same time. But, she looked at me and I looked at her, and just then my heart overtook my tears and they flowed hard. This baby girl and I could tackle anything thrown at us, together. She was long and breathtakingly beautiful with dark hair and blue eyes. She grabbed my hand and put it directly into her mouth.

Welcome to the world, Riley Ann.

Michael gasped inquisitively at her ear, it had an imperfection. Her ear had not attached to her head while she was in my womb, and as I gazed at her, in disbelief that she didn't have Down's and searching for signs; the ear was the least of my concerns. I scowled at him and told him she was perfect and he shook it off and stared too. He kissed me on the cheek and sported his "Riley's Daddy" T-shirt his mom and I made, and followed her to the nursery. When they left, I sat in awe of all I had just done. I had fought so long to have a healthy baby and to have this moment and it was all worth it.

Michael and I disagreed about a lot of things, one of which was her name. Michael wanted Petra or some other ridiculous name honoring his Italian/Irish/Polish heritage and I was sold on Mackenzie, until I found the name Riley. We had settled on Riley and allowed our families to decide how we were going to spell it. I wanted the traditional Irish way and he wanted to fancy it up. That Christmas Eve before she was born, we wrote down all the different ways we liked to spell her name and let our families decide how to spell it. I also won this one with my votes being solid and my influence taking over. When I looked at her, I was glad I chose Riley, she didn't look like a

Mackenzie, a Petra or a Bella, she looked like a Riley. She looked like a perfect little pink miracle. This tiny person we created and I grew in my belly had saved my life and I would spend the rest of mine proving how worthy I was of her and how loved she is. A few hours after her arrival, that same midwife that cared for me and cried with me walked into my recovery room to say hi. Unfortunately, she did not deliver Riley because it was her day off, but when she heard Riley was here, she came to see her. I will never be able to truly convey my admiration, respect and affection for Christine, but I hope that this simple "thank you" will tell her exactly how special she is to my family and I.

Well, Michael and I set out to go home with our new miracle. She had latched on like a champ, was healthy, except for a minor bout with jaundice that was fixed after a few days of our discharge home under lamps and labs, and cute as a button so homebound we were. It was in those first few moments as a family that I was blissfully happy and somehow knew it would never last. Michael and I enjoyed the first few weeks of parenthood, in a happy marriage. He was cautious and gentle with Riley and I was a seasoned mom, so I instantly felt confident.

Riley was two weeks old and it was Easter weekend, she was vomiting painfully and projectiling across the room. My child was struggling and it was painful to watch as she forcefully threw up my milk and couldn't hold it down. I called the Pediatrician, she and I had known each other for a decade now and she knew I only called when it was vital. Her partner was on call and he called me back and said let's give her some Pedialite and I will call you back in the morning and check on her. The pain was horrible in my breasts as I became engorged, but it was nothing compared to watching my Riley struggle.

The next morning, at 8am the doctor called and Riley was no better so he told me to take her to the Emergency Room. I was terrified. What was wrong? Was it my milk? What was it? I tried to wake Michael up and tell him to come with us and he wouldn't get up. He said he'd be there later. I was so astonished that he was not more concerned about his infant daughter having to go to the Emergency Room. I packed her up and woke Kayla up, she wanted to stay home, so I told her Michael was there and when he came up to the hospital to be ready so she could go too.

That entire day was specific and went by like molasses for me. Michael's amazing father came up to sit with me, his mother had the Flu and Kayla was home with my sleeping husband who couldn't be bothered to pull himself out of bed to go to the hospital with his new baby. I called incessantly and begged him to come to the hospital, with each call he got more angry and vicious, so I stopped. I would call and check on Kayla instead. I was alone, terrified and angry and he was asleep. I was left to handle and care for our child in her time of need while for him, sleeping and being verbally abusive were more important. My last call was to say we were getting discharged, that Riley had to see a specialist for reflux and Kayla answered the phone crying. I was unsure what had gone on, so I asked her to explain and she said she was hungry and Michael wouldn't get up and make her anything so she tried to make popcorn and it burned. Michael smelled it and got out of bed to scold her and he was now up and pissed. I told her I was on my way and would stop and get food for everyone. I walked in armed with Mama Bear courage and utter disappointment in my husband, the man that vowed for better and for worse to me; this was worse and he was absent. I endured an eight hour day with my infant child in the emergency room having test after test and starving, while he slept at home and verbally berated and belittled my eldest child. I peed one time during that whole day and it was because I begged a pediatric nurse to come and hold Riley so that I could pee. Her father should have been there holding her, holding me and just being there for this monumental moment in her life.

I came in, put Riley down and gave Kayla her food. I quietly told her to eat and went to talk to Michael. I asked why he was being so rude to Kayla and he couldn't understand why I believed her over him, which to me was so juvenile. After some nasty comments and words, I grabbed my children and left. I was so hurt he couldn't be bothered to care about his child's wellbeing but instead chose to destroy my child's psyche while I was gone. We walked to the car and he began to scream obscenities at me and Kayla and told me I was not leaving with the car he bought me. Kayla was terrified I was going to go to jail for taking my car and Michael began to throw rocks at me while I loaded

Riley into the car. I was now afraid, but my focus was getting my kids out of there safely. We loaded up and he ran back inside, I thought we were going to end up in a car chase. He stayed home and I went to Marie's house, Riley's Godmother, where he called and harassed me. Marie asked if I thought he was doing drugs again, and I didn't know there was a first time; this was how I found out. Apparently, drug abuse was his thing and our relationship had been the longest since he had used. Now his need to sleep all day and be so hateful to Kayla and I was making sense to me. Eventually, after a few hours, I went home. I walked in and he was once again sleeping and I tucked the kids in and began to decorate for Easter morning. I sat in the dark and filled Easter baskets and hid eggs and went off to bed. I wanted to be sure he was fast asleep before I went in and I quietly cried myself to sleep in our marital bed. I prayed that Riley slept through the night so as not to wake him and have to deal with all his uncertainty. I hadn't felt that alone since that first instance with Terrell many moons prior.

Slowly and almost all at once, we began fighting all the time. Each fight got more aggressive in the words and actions until the day came when he finally did what we could never come back from for good. It was early morning and he was supposed to get up and take Kayla to school, but he was hungover and sleeping on the couch. I yelled to him to wake up from the bedroom and he didn't. I was breastfeeding Riley and I got up from our bed and went to the living room and bopped him on the head to wake up. He jumped up so fast and got in my face and told me he would knock my teeth out of my mouth if I talked to him again. I didn't back down. I knew he wouldn't touch me while I was holding her and she was feeding; I was wrong. He pushed me out of his way and yelled at Kayla so mean and aggressive telling her to get in the car. I was not having him drive her to school and I grabbed the keys and headed towards the car with Riley still feeding. He grabbed my hair and told me he was doing it now that I had woken him up. I calmly asked him to go back inside and I would take her. My neighbor walked out while all the yelling he was doing was going on and Michael went inside. I left and cried after I dropped Kayla off at school. I didn't go back to the house, I went to my Aunt's house and just said I was there for a visit. But, she knew something was wrong since I was in my pajamas and hair up in a bun. When I got home he was getting ready to leave for work. He never apologized, he never acknowledged that happened, nothing. He just left and didn't even say goodbye to Riley.

He never did anything to me physically like Terrell did, and he knew what Terrell did to me, he hated it and then became what he promised he never would. He was verbally abusive and he did other things to make me feel small and alone; his words were harsh and cut deep. He slapped me, and held me down and pushed me, but those were no where close to what Terrell did to me physically. His words destroyed me and whatever confidence I had rebuilt. He would tell me I was a fat cow or fat bitch and that no one would ever want me again. And because I didn't want to shave my vagina bald for him, he would call me a hairy fat cow or hairy fat bitch. I have never understood why a man is attracted to a bald vagina, it is a child's vagina then. I get the desire to have no hair and the ease of navigating the terrain, but if you think about a woman, she has hair. Now, I'm not saying that we as women should have 1960's style bush, but something is better than nothing at our ages. Pubic hair growth is how we know we are becoming a woman. Why are we trying to revert back to childhood with that? As someone that has been molested as a child, I have trouble with it, real trouble. Before you go thinking I have this long luxurious bush, sorry, I don't. I am still a woman and want to be trimmed and maintained down there.

Anyhow, off topic I went. Michael made me feel the way he talked to me. He made me feel incapable and weak and I was not. In late September that year, I got very sick and went to my doctor who then sent me to the emergency room where I found out I needed my gallbladder out and my intestines were blocked. Michael had to be home with the girls and take care of them, plus bring Riley up to me every day so that she could stimulate my milk and I could pump. On one of these five days that I was there, Michael was incredibly angry saying he hadn't slept in days but his mom was staying at our house helping with the kids, so I couldn't understand why he was so tired. Shit I never got that kind of help from her. She and I used to be incredibly close, until I had Riley and she tried to tell me how to mother my baby. She had always told me how to mother her baby, but this one was mine and I didn't need her input. She was insufferably involved in Michael's life and our marriage and I finally had to put my foot down when it came to Riley. I may not have been a great wife, but I was an excellent mother and frankly she was not one I wanted advice on parenting from; her son was a trainwreck. This same woman also took it upon herself to rearrange my kitchen because it worked better her way. So, clearly I was not ok with her being there when I was not and did not want her help. So, now more than a decade later, she still holds a grudge I think, but we are cordial for Riley. Mind you her granddaughter is an honor student and incredibly well behaved, but I am a bitch so I am just horrible and there is no coming back from that.

Whoops, off topic again. Anyway, Michael brought the girls up to the hospital to see me and Kayla was hungry so he took her down to the cafeteria while my cousin Jared and Riley and I stayed in my room. Jared played with Riley and I soaked up every minute I got with her. Pretty soon after they leave, Kayla comes in crying and tells Jared and I why she was. Jared is Kayla's Godfather and the only father she ever knew, so he is pretty protective of her. He was getting quite angry listening to her story. She said that Michael was yelling at her downstairs in the cafeteria about her milk she left in the cereal bowl, telling her she had to drink it. She didn't want to drink it, so he grabbed her by the neck and made her drink it. Jared told me he was going to lay him out as soon as he walked in and I told him to go and take Kayla, that I would handle it. He came in and was angry and said, "Oh I am sure you believe her." I was baffled, he was doing this victim shit again against a ten year old. I told him to take Riley and go home. Jared had Kayla and he could come back and pick me up the next day but Kayla would not be home until I was.

I got home from the surgery and things were extremely rocky. Michael and I barely spoke, we hadn't had sex in months and he was drinking consistently all the time. I was, in the end, actually glad to find out his mom had been there to help, because at least I knew my girls were safe. About ten days after I got home, the shit hit the fan and my marriage was over. We fought terribly that night about things that I cannot remember.

What I remember was him packing his things and pushing me so hard into Kayla and her arm getting stuck in my bed rails. I remember him spitting in my face and slapping me. I felt so completely enraged and hurt at the same time. I remember him walking down the hall and me throwing a bottle of No Tears at his head and landing it. I remember him running back down the hall like a crazed lunatic and picking me up and throwing me on the bed. I remember my kids watching it all. Riley standing in her crib, Kayla laying crying on the bed and now I was next to her.

Kayla ran to her room and called the police and I called his father. They both showed up at the same time and the officer was his friend and then we had his father there. He politicianed his son right out of jail and out of the house. The deputy, who was at our wedding, asked me what I wanted to happen and I said I want him gone and I want him to never come back. It was done. We were done. We had both crossed that line that you can't come back from. Our marriage was over and I was not pretending anymore.

When the dust settled and I put the kids to bed, I went to pack his shit. In that packing of his stuff I found his drugs, the reason he was no longer the man I married. He was an addict and an alcoholic and had now ruined our family. I found comfort in the girls. I found understanding in my neighbors. They were these island cousins that had been there before we moved in and were so nice to the girls and I; Kayla adored them. They looked out for us and helped me carry in groceries and strollers and fixed broken vacuums and light bulbs. We

tried to be cordial to each other for Riley's sake. I let him come over
for Riley's first Christmas morning, which was the year of my ghetto
Christmas tree. I made my red living room curtains, our Christmas
tree because I had no money for a tree. I had no idea how I would even
be able to take care of Christmas for my girls, but I prayed and it all
was able to come together. It was nothing glorious, but that was and is
not the point of the holiday so I didn't mind it much. My girls never
knew the struggle, or worry, and that was what it is supposed to be
like.

My divorce became final after a short time mediating our desires, on
April Fools day, only six and a half months after Michael left. I came
home with a bottle of rum and wanted to celebrate. I was free of my
marriage and Michael was no longer my problem, he would be
someone else's addict now. I struggled with this part and wasn't sure
if I should include it, but I am being authentically myself, so there it
goes. My neighbor, Jose, was this incredibly sexy ex boxer. He had a
smile that would drop your panties and muscles that would hold you
securely. Shortly after Michael left, Jose fractured his hand and I
helped him get to the Doctor and took care of him after he came home
from surgery. We were getting closer and becoming better friends. We
had flirted back and forth over the time I was married, but innocently,
never anything more than a quick smile or wink or nice compliment; I
was a married woman. Now, I am no longer married. Jose was working
on his car like he always was, when I pulled up divorce decree in hand.
I was elated. You have to understand how free I felt. I didn't work after
Riley was born, and when Michael left, he left me with no money, so I
had to ask him for every piece of food that was brought into that
house. He told me if I wanted groceries to sell my wedding band, so I

did. He was cruel to me and when I stepped out of that car, Jose was there with his same smile. He helped me get Riley out of the car, like he did every day, and asked me if I was divorced now. I looked into his dark brown eyes and said yes! He helped me get the girls in the house and went home. I fed the girls, chatted with some friends on the phone and put the kids down for bed. There was a knock at the door and it was Jose with a bottle of Rum for me and some coke. I smiled and invited him in and made us a drink. We talked and laughed and drank our Rum, then he went home. The next few weeks we hung out more and more and then Michael had Riley and Kayla was with friends and Jose came over and we had sex. It was mind blowing. It was just what I needed and just the one time. He was not the only person I slept with in Michael and I's marital bed, the other was this hot shot young and HOT firefighter that was friends with Michael. I had known him because he worked at the same place Michael did and during my pregnancy he would bring me over a sundae from Baskin Robbins every now and then to hang out with Michael. Now, I wonder if he had a crush on me the whole time and that was why he came over, but I will never know. One night I was out at a bar my friends would hang out at and he was there.We spoke and he asked for my number and I never thought he would call. I thought he was trying to make an older woman feel good because he did. But, a week later he called and then we began chatting and one day he called me on his way back from Orlando and asked if he could come over. I was like sure, I had no expectations, and was not really sure what we were doing. But, he came over and when I opened the front door, he grabbed me with one arm and began kissing me and closed the door with the other. Then in one swoop I was in the air and he was carrying me to my room and it was some sexy shit what he did. He had carried me from the front door to the bedroom and he fucked me the way you would imagine a young twenty something firemen would do. He made me feel desired and sexy and I needed that. He was definitely worth it and I didn't feel anything but sexy that day and the day with Jose. These two men that knew my husband found me sexy and my husband was disgusted by me, and that was ok by me. It was just what I needed.

Chapter Eighteen

My Sweet Nuggie

*D*uring Riley's beginnings, she didn't have the easiest start. Difficult pregnancy for me, early birth for her followed by jaundice and then reflux. After that Emergency Room visit, I took Riley to the Gastroenterologist and I found out then that her little anus was not quite opened and he had to manually stretch it in the doctor's office because she was having difficulty pooping; again, I did this alone. Every major milestone in Riley's life, he wasn't there for, sadly. When she was about four months old, Michael was home and normal that night and I went in to take a shower and he was playing with Riley. When I came out, he asked me if she had always had that big bump on her forehead. I had noticed it, but didn't think anything of it. So, when he pointed it out, now I got worried. I got her into the Pediatrician the next day and she told me that it looked like her forehead hadn't fused together properly and we should watch it for the next few months, and see if it gets better. She also told me that she noticed Riley wasn't turning her neck to look around, she stayed focused in one direction. So, she set us up to have physical therapy at home for her, for what she said was torticollis. The therapist came one day and showed me what I needed to do for her and how to accomplish the goals and then it was up to me and Michael to fix this.

He worked all day, so I did the exercises with her to strengthen her neck, all while that same bump stayed there, just staring at me daily. The pediatrician referred us to a plastic surgeon a few months later, she didn't want to say what she thought it was and be incorrect, but she wanted to be thorough, so off we went.

We sat in this basic office separated at this point and heading for divorce, with our baby and a bunch of little children's toys and photos on the wall of all of the cleft palate repairs that this skilled plastic surgeon had done. Then, they called in our baby girl. We went back with a very pleasant and patient nurse and she took images of Riley's head and its shape and then waited for the doctor. Dr. Eric Stelnicki walked in, every ounce of confidence,warmth, kindness and knowledge a scared mom could want. He sat with Michael and I and answered question after question and nestled Riley while she napped in his arms checking her skull out. He told us she had plagiocephaly, which is basically that her head is flat due to position or pressure on the spots of the head. She had multiple spots that were that way, hence the lump on her forehead. The treatment for this is a helmet to shape the soft skull before it begins to harden, that's why you see babies with these helmets and not toddlers. He said based on the scans, she would have to wear it for up to 6 months 23 hours a day! I was baffled, we live in Florida, the hottest place and I have to make her wear this helmet in that heat. Michael and I left and went our separate ways and I couldn't help but blame myself for her predicament.

I used to work at the place that made these helmets when I was 19, so I wanted to take her there. I made the appointment and Michael and I went together. They came in and discussed how they would make the mold of Riley's head with plaster and answered questions. I sat there holding my baby while an orthotist applied plaster pieces to her beautiful head and she had to sit there with that plaster on while it hardened. She was so excellent sitting on my lap, smiling at the Orthotist and removing her pacy to smile bigger and coo at us all. After some time, the plaster hardened and it was time to remove the cast and pick out the design. Her nursery bedding was purple with butterflies and they had a purple butterfly design, so that was it! We made a follow up appointment for the helmet fitting and then we went to leave. The helmet was quite costly and Michael and I didn't have that kind of money, so we turned to his parents to help pay for it. His dad paid for the entire helmet, no questions asked. Michael's dad is the hardest part of our divorce, he is truly a genuine man with a great heart and love for Riley. He would do absolutely anything for his princess. Michael and I took Riley to get her ears pierced because I wanted to have her have them before the helmet in case it was 6 months that she had to wear it. She was only nine months old when she got the helmet and I couldn't imagine holding a toddler down for an ear piercing.

So, helmet day comes, Riley's ears are sporting pretty diamonds and her helmet is covered in beautiful butterflies. We have to go back every week and have it adjusted as her head begins to fill in the gaps. They basically shave down the inside where she is filling it in and shaping her skull. The ordeal of that helmet was dreadful to watch for her. She wasn't crawling yet because of her torticollis and probably that heavy helmet, so she just sat in the room and scooted on her butt everywhere. When she got to take the helmet off for that hour a day, she would dig at her scalp and scratch it. The thing smelled and the only way to wash it was in her bath with her. She hated it but boy was she adorable in it. Riley only had to wear it for two months; she got it off right before her first birthday.

Riley hasn't had it easy since birth, but she is resilient and stronger than she believes she is.

Chapter Nineteen

I want seasons alright!

*T*he week before we leave to move to North Carolina, I
arrange to meet Michael to discuss Riley and the move. He tells me
that day that he spent most of our marriage on drugs and he was
going to rehab once we leave and he would be unreachable for the
three weeks that rehab was. I begged him to be better for Riley
because she deserved it. We left and moved to North Carolina and I
knew it would give the girls and I a better life. The following month,
Riley was turning two. We hadn't spoken to Michael because he was in
rehab and I went ahead and planned her birthday and he was
supposed to come up for it. I was extremely hesitant about him
coming because he was going to stay at the same house I was staying
at with our friends and I had found out that he never actually made it
past two days in rehab. I didn't know what sort of shape he was in and
that made me more nervous. The day had come for him to be here and
he walked in the door and Riley looked at him and ran into my arms
scared, he had lost like 100 pounds since we had been gone and didn't
look the same. Drugs had taken over his life and had him lose so much
weight that he was unrecognizable.

The next day we went to Riley's daycare for a little birthday
celebration and he rode with me. He sat in the corner, sweating,
judging and complaining the entire time. After her little friends sang

Happy Birthday and they ate cupcakes and danced around, we took Riley to go home. We went to leave and Riley was throwing a fit because she didn't want to leave and get in her carseat. I am struggling with her to get her in, every parent knows this terrible two year old fit, and Michael is very concerned with her runny nose and trying to wipe it. I turn and say, "that can wait Michael" and he didn't like that so he became an asshole cursing at me in the daycare parking lot. I got Riley in and got in myself and started to drive, Michael went to light a cigarette in my car and I didn't smoke with Riley in the car and I was not smoking in the car as it was. So, I told him there is no smoking in my car, he said "FUCK YOU!" I locked the windows and he pulled his fist back to punch me in the face while I was driving and Riley screamed, then he grabbed the steering wheel and Riley was screaming. Something in him let go and I told him he had to be out of the house when we got back because I was not sleeping anywhere he was and we were living there now.

At some point, Michael cleaned himself up and moved up to North Carolina after Riley's third birthday. He began to see her regularly and in the beginning she didn't want to go and then it got easier for her to go. Michael was living with Marie, Riley's godmother at this point and he was letting Marie do the mothering things for him and it irritated me. He has never really taken on his parental responsibility and that was all I wanted him to do, that was what she deserved. He lasted in North Carolina a few years and then the reality of looking for work and not being able to hold down a job became too much to handle.

He called me one Thursday in February and told me that he was moving back to Florida with his parents and he was leaving on Tuesday. I couldn't believe it. I told him that we should tell her together, at this point she was in First Grade and almost seven and she was pretty smart. I wanted us to tell her together so that her questions would be fully answered, he agreed. Saturday morning comes and it is her weekend at home with me and Michael calls. She puts him on speaker, like she always does, and he asks Riley if she wants to come see him that day and Riley said "no daddy, it's mommy time." He immediately responded in anger demanding, "well, I don't know when you will see me then because I'm moving back to Florida on Tuesday!" The look on her face was as if he had just kicked her in the stomach and stole her favorite doll. This destroyed her. She was caught between wanting to see her dad and wanting to be with me. She decided not to go to see him and I tried to encourage her to go but she was having none of that.

Off to Florida he went, and into therapy shortly after she went. The kid was angry and confused and fearful to tell her dad how she felt about anything. She was having a deep internal struggle with being angry and him being her father and she wasn't dealing with the anger appropriately. I became her anger focus and it was hard for me, but her therapist told me she was projecting her anger on me because I was a safe space for it. Riley is normally the most empathetic child, dripping in kindness and now she was angry and frustrated all the time. Slowly, she began to open up to me and her therapist about her anger, sadness and the loss she was feeling; things began to change in her too. She started to be more confident and assertive almost overnight it seemed. She spoke up to me about everything she disagreed with, lord help me; but still not to her dad. After about a year in therapy, he was coming to town to visit her and Riley wanted him to come to her therapy while he was there. In that room, on the floor playing games as a family with her therapist gently directing Riley; she opened up. She told her dad why she was hurt and why she was angry with him. I was so proud of her strength and honesty, but her dad had nothing but excuses and explanations, instead of just hearing her and embracing her courage. I realized that day that we can't expect people to respond to things the same way that we want or hope for, we have to accept them just where they are and not try and change them. I stopped being angry with how he responded to things that day and how he handled our daughter. I just knew that I had to be the parent she deserved always and support everything she dreamt about and always listen in a way that she would speak to me. North Carolina changed this grouchy, aggressive mean Miamian into a softer more thoughtful mom without me realizing it. I came here originally for a fresh start and to give my girls better schools and neighborhoods. I have stayed because this is the only place that I have felt most like me in. I am content in the winters and thrilled in the summers. The luxury of seeing seasons and experiencing the gorgeous colors of fall is worth leaving my home for. Miami will always be home, my roots are there and my soul is there, but my heart is here.

Chapter Twenty

A Flair for The Dramatics

*E*veryone that knew my mom knew that she had a sense

for the flair and dramatics, I wonder where I learned that from! From coming up with elaborate April Fools hoaxes to her daily practical jokes and dramatic stories you never really knew what was reality and what was theatrics. Like I know without a doubt that my mom loved me, but some of her stories are unbelievable, literally. My mom has told me multiple stories about my birth mother and father, each one different depending on her mood or motivation. One version is that my mother was very young, like 16 when she had me and she couldn't raise me so she gave me to the Catholic Nuns. Another is that my parents were in love and married but in college and unable to care for me so they drove to Florida from New York to have me and give me over to the Catholic Nuns. The other one I got was that my mom was a college student that met my dad on a trip to Puerto Rico and they weren't together so she gave me up for adoption and her parents never knew; in this one she was 25. It is pretty difficult to figure out who you are when you have no idea where you came from and what story is actually true.

Why have I never asked my dad? Great question, I have asked him though, and he doesn't remember, apparently. But he can remember that I was a sick baby that threw up all over the place and that is what made him fall in love with me and not give me back. Who knows what is fact and what is fiction. There is another story that has always had me wondering. Apparently, before my birth parents were to sign the official papers giving me up for adoption, they asked for some time with me. My dad came to the adoption agency a little early and saw them. He said I look just like her now, my mom, and she was very tall and my dad was short. This has haunted me since he told me. These people that created me are somewhere out there and I have no idea who they are and what they look like and why they didn't raise me. I used to walk around on South Beach almost certain that I would encounter a woman that looked just like me and had beautiful black long flowing hair. I fantasized that the instant I found her she would tell me that she was so sorry and ask for forgiveness and to be in my life. She would tell me that she was going to take me to meet my dad and we would walk off with her arm around me. I fantasized about a life that was not filled with rape and molestation. One where I could just be a normal kid. I used to wonder what my life would have been like had they just raised me, but I never go down that rabbit hole. It is a slippery slope that is dangerous to me mentally. My life would be different but my girls would not exist and I can't imagine a world where they aren't. So, instead I wear the rape, molestation and abuse daily and try to heal somehow.

So when my mom told me the story about them adopting Lizy, I questioned it too. The story goes that Mark was an only child and asked for a sister and they took him to the orphanage and he "picked out" Lizy in a crib to be his sister. Um...I find that strange and romanticized for effect. I am not sure about the actual story, but the greater question I had was, did Mark even want a sister? He isn't a big brother to either of us, so did he? I can count on one hand the only time he was a big brother to me, that was when he took me to see my mom in the hospital and when I was pregnant with Kayla. Otherwise he was off doing his own thing and being anything but brotherly. I made my peace with my lack of sibling interest a long time ago, just another thing that I will not have. My stepmother made sure to poison them all against me, with her half truths and poor intentions. I mean what parent tries to get the other siblings on their side? What kind of parent does this to a child that she was aware was part of the package getting my dad? She is trash. She is toxic. As I am writing this book, the final straw has occurred with regards to the parental units.

It is a Monday, and I am driving home from work in terrible Charlotte traffic. Riley calls me and says that there is a big box on the front porch from Grandpa, I immediately think of my ex-husbands dad, not mine. I tell her when I get home I will carry it in. Sure enough, I pull up and there is a big box sitting there. I carry it inside and notice it is from my dad; I was shocked. The only time in my adult life I got a package from my dad was when he gave me a laptop years ago, so this big box had my curiosity peaked. I put it on the kitchen table and went to the bathroom. Riley yelled something from the kitchen about opening it and I said sure. I came out to find her holding an envelope with my step monster's handwriting on it that read, "Shit 1997-2004" I literally had no words. I was stunned. Riley was very confused and asked, "why would grandma write that about you?" I told her I don't know, but I was sure it was a mistake and closed the box and brought it into my room. Clearly to me, this was a box of maliciousness and hate. This was not the innocent memories box my dad had me believe based on his typed letter, not handwritten, typed and no warmth or love at all. No, Love Dad, just Dad. Unreal. Just then, I realized that I had been begging for my dad to notice me. Begging for him to actually want to be my dad and he has no interest in it or me. Much like his disinterest in being a grandfather to my children. The gifts and cards over the years came from her, not him. The lack of interest in my children always baffled me.

My kids were intelligent, witty and warm; everything they should be and they too have to fight for their attention. Eventually, Kayla made her own choice that she didn't want to partake in their dance of manipulation any longer, and I wholeheartedly believe that Riley will come to the same acceptance soon enough. They spend 3 measly hours a year with her for a non-personal lunch. They don't make any effort to see Riley, spend time with her, or even get to know her. My step monster believes that Riley should be contacting them, that they don't have to call her. To me and my therapist, that is ludacris. Riley is a child she cannot be expected to keep up with communications; I had to remind her dad of the same. When Riley is with her father, I call her, I don't expect her to call me. These morons think that the sun rises and sets in their assholes and a tween should be responsible for maintaining a relationship with them. Not to mention that my parental units normally live in Miami, but for 6 months out of the year, they reside in NC a mere 2 hours away. Hmm...you would think that they would make more of an effort. But, their friends and running club are more important and keeping up the appearance of being fantastic grandparents means more to them.

Now with my sister's kid, they are grandparents. Every ounce of what my children deserved and never got. The monster will say it is because I kept the girls away, but that is not accurate. My ex-husband took Riley to them in Miami for Christmas one year and Riley's godmother takes her to them so they can exercise their 3 hours a year visit; to clear their consciences. The monster did so much irreparable damage to Kayla's psyche with her belittling comments about her weight and calories she eats, that I fear she will do that same thing to Riley. If she ever does, that is the end of their relationship. Riley has this magnificent body confidence at merely twelve years old, that I wish I had. She is comfortable in her own skin, and feels beautiful just the way she is. If I have done one thing right in my life, it is her view of her body and I pray every day that it always stays that way. Kayla had that same view, until the monster started making comments here and there and they stuck. Much like me being "unlovable" or "an orphan" words from loved ones stay with us and leave damaging imperfections that cannot go away.

Anyhow, in this box of bullshit was the most treasured thing that I could have ever given my dad. When I was in second grade, I entered a Father's Day Writing contest with the Miami Herald and my writing was published there as a runner up. I mentioned this earlier in the story. I didn't win, but I was so proud of that article. The monster had it professionally framed and it hung in my dad's office for years and then somehow, it got into my bedroom on the wall by the door. Every time I walked out of that room, I looked at it. Every time I was angry with my dad or slammed my bedroom door, it was there. This pink frame, clearly she never knew me at all- I hate pink, that just hung there reminding me every day of the bond between my father and I that she couldn't destroy. He had chosen me and I wore that so proudly and intently that no one could take that from me. When Riley was not around, I peaked back in the box of hate and there sticking out a little bit was a pink wooden worn frame. My heart sank into my stomach.

My throat swelled up and I mustered every ounce of courage I had left in me and pulled out what I knew would not be that article. I was wrong. I was defeated. That was the final straw. Everything else in that box was straight bullshit from the monster to me showing me that one last time she could say fuck you without being in front of me. I waited a few days, went to my weekly therapy and talked about it. I talked to Samantha and Traci too. Everyone was in awe of the contents of this box and it's true intent and I needed to know. It was like a cancer in my blood eating away at me for days. Why now send this box when we haven't spoken or seen each other in a year. Why? So, I sat down and wrote them both an email. Expressing my hurt, anger and disbelief. It was liberating and released me from the questions I had, even if they never responded or did, I was free from the pain; so I thought. Almost immediately, I get a disgusting hateful text from the monster and an email from my father. You see I had told them that they were not allowed to make plans to see Riley any longer without discussing it with me. Currently, they had been doing this through Riley's god mother and let's face it, while Riley sees her as family, she is not legally and not able to make decisions for my child. This has gone on long enough and I was finally strong enough to put a stop to it. I told them that they were welcome to see her whenever they wanted, they just had to arrange it with me first. The monster did not like that. She told me she would never check with me first to see "her granddaughter." She was insane if she thought I would allow it without me knowing. I made that choice last year after they almost killed themselves and my kid on one of their visits. They took her to Sliding Rock and well, Riley slid in and then, in went her godmother trying to save Riley, and then in went the monster trying to save them and then my dad went in to get them all out. It was terrifying for Riley and she was scared and nervous. She is not adventurous at all. I was not told they were doing this. If something had happened to Riley I would not even know where to look since I had no itinerary, shit even her dad has to give me that, why would they be any different?

I wasn't even told that they fell in until after Riley had eaten dinner with them and drove the two hours back home. Well, my dad's response was something like "what a spectacular misread on your part" and "for you to impute evil is your problem not mine." Followed by my personal favorite, "Are you so self-centered to think that I would spend one second of my precious time planning how to be evil and/or hurt you? Do you lack self-awareness? Must you always project your own shortcomings on everyone who has ever been close to you? Will you ever let go of your self-hatred?" My dad claims he knew nothing about the contents, he says that he asked the bitch what it was and she said "shit from the Royal Palm days" and he thought it was items I would want back. When I lived in Royal Palm Apartments, is what she is referring to; I was 21 and a single mom struggling to make it, and moved back to Miami to be closer to my parents and sister so that they could help me with Kayla. I made some really poor decisions during that time in my life and got us evicted from that apartment.

This was during the time that I was in a relationship with Lester and we moved to Tampa. I grabbed what I could and left the apartment before they could change the locks. When they called my parents, who's name was also on the lease, to come and clean it out, my step mother claims that I left it a disaster. She and I have *very* different views of this situation, she even took photos of how much disarray I left behind, yet when Lester and I left, we also took a photo together with Kayla and there was no such mess, so I am pretty sure she trashed the place in another attempt at attention and sympathy. So, inside this box of pure evil were those photos of my destruction, many many emails back and forth between her and my dad talking about what an utter disappointment and nightmare I was to them and my article. The emails, and bank books didn't faze me because, let's be honest, I was a twenty-one year old child and my dad gave me a bank account for emergencies and I used it and he didn't like it. I overdrew it, I admit that, but there was absolutely no need to include your correspondence with the Suntrust bank president about your troubled daughter.

Again, just to inflict pain and further prove your hatred. So, they received my email back and what ensued next was comical to say the least. Daddy claimed that Sandy knew what was in the box and it was all the stuff from the apartment, yet my article was in there at the bottom of the box. The same article that hung on the wall when my 4 year old Riley came to that house and you showed it to her. But wait, the Royal Palm days were when I was 21 years old, I didn't even have Riley then.

So, who is the liar, daddy or the bitch? Your guess is the same as mine, the bitch. She claims that she told my dad that she had no idea what was in those boxes. HA! LIAR! This box's intentions are truly unknown, but one thing is for certain, it delivered a world of hurt with every single item I pulled out. I still haven't gone through the entire thing. A large portion of it sits in my therapist's office because I am just not ready to look at hatred items nor do I want that kind of negativity in my life.

I am truly disappointed in my dad. I told him that the article was included and he didn't ask for it back, he didn't question it's validity, he didn't even respond after that. Message received daddy, I am no longer your little grease monkey. I am no longer your little sickly girl. I am truly the orphan you told me I was many years ago. Yes, I remember you telling me I didn't deserve your last name and I was an orphan. Super! Just what I always wanted to hear from my lifelong hero and now disappointment. When those words of hatred were written to me with a pure intent of inflicting pain towards your daughter, I changed once again. I went from a little girl searching and seeking her fathers love, approval and admiration to a woman that didn't give a shit about any of it. A woman that knew I was not the problem, you were. A woman that no longer needed your validation, support or love. You made it super clear on numerous occasions how you feel towards me and about me and that you never wanted to be a father. Not sure I should've ever been told that, but whatevs, I was. And you all thought I was being dramatic about my parents, ha!

They are just as bad as I have portrayed them. I was actually quite kind in that portrayal, and I owe them nothing. I will always hold out hope that one day, my father will realize what a manipulator she has been to him and want a relationship with me; but then again, I still think there is a chance for me to have a fairytale love, so delusional, party of 1 your table is ready.

Chapter Twenty-One

The life changer

*I*n my early thirties, I worked at an oncology practice. It was the most rewarding and difficult job I had ever had. During that time, there was a girl there that I worked with that changed my life and another that made my life better. Let's start with the one that made my life better. Her name was Allison, she was ambitious, intelligent and poised, but able to cut up and laugh. She was what I imagined I would be as a manager. She told me about the college she went to online and how it fit into her schedule and allowed her to get her MBA and work. I had always dreamed of going to college from being a little girl, so this sounded like the way I could do it. I met with a counselor over the phone and enrolled in February of 2012, it was the best decision I had made for myself. I felt so positive and looked toward my future as a college grad. Allison was kind enough to proctor my tests, help me study and just be there for me during the beginning of this journey.

It was quite difficult balancing a full time job, being a single mom and now a full time student too. I studied on lunch breaks, in between patients and long after the girls went to bed; I was determined. In all that determination and positivity, came exhaustion and a lack of self care. On August 20, 2012 I had the beginning of a four day migraine and one of the worst I had to date. I went to work and pushed through it barely being able to see out of my eye and being exhausted. I was in the middle of taking English II and my instructor was awesome. I absolutely loved his classes and found that this week I was unable to enjoy them.

On Thursday that week, I had to be at a different office and then go to an administrative meeting with the hospital system we worked for. While I was there, I got incredibly dizzy and almost instantly while talking to one of the nurses, I saw the floor coming towards me. I was about to pass out and she grabbed me and sat me in a chair and gave me a soda to drink. I began to feel better and stood up to go to the meeting. I was driving with someone else so that was good because I didn't feel 100%. During the meeting, the seating that was provided had me turned around the whole thing looking at the screen and my neck was hurting. When we left the meeting, I felt nauseated and different. I just wanted to get in my car and drive to the other office. I left, headed towards the interstate and got on one exchange leading to the main one I needed to be on. When I merged there onto I-77, it would be about a 15 mile drive to my office. I merged and I remember nothing else from that moment. I pulled into my office parking lot terribly and walked in confused and looking for the nurse I worked with. I told her something was wrong and I needed her help.

She immediately put me in a chemo chair and took my blood pressure, which was 154/100. That is extremely high for me, so I was concerned, but I couldn't verbalize that. She went to get the doctor I worked for and he came quickly and checked me out. He told her I needed to go to the ER and since it was right down the street a few blocks she could take me instead of waiting on an ambulance. He told her he thought I had a seizure or something because I was so confused. We got to the ER and that amazing nurse I worked with, Susie, never left my side. I was given a CT and two lumbar punctures and they couldn't find anything wrong. They said I needed to be admitted since I had the lumbar puncture and I had to be monitored. Once I got into my hospital room, the hospitalist doctor came in to evaluate and take some medical history. She was kind and young and wore a shelled necklace. I was familiar with those since I grew up in Miami and spent a lot of time in The Keys. She told me that because I was so confused still, she wanted to get an MRI to be sure there wasn't anything else going on. So, off to the MRI I went the next morning. She came in a few hours later and sat next to me on the bed, held my hand and said the sentence that changed my life, "I don't know how to tell you this, but you had a stroke." A lot of important and traumatizing statements in my life have started that way, "I don't know how to tell you this but..." I remember looking at her, confused while the tears ran down my face and the fear washed over me. I knew this fear, it was paralyzing and overwhelming. It was the fear of death I had known during my relationship with Terrell. I did not survive violence twice and unspeakable acts done against me to now die; and it was my own brain betraying me. I sat and listened to her tell me the next steps, and I can't honestly tell you what she said. I was in shock. I was terrified and at a loss for words. What would this mean for my kids and for me? What was my life going to be like? Every person that I had seen with a stroke or heard about either had terrible deficits or they died. I had zero time to die and I did not need any deficits. I laid in that hospital bed, quietly sobbing and praying. I was alone with my thoughts and fears and they overwhelmed me. Shortly after, my friend Sarah (the other person that changed my life at that job) showed up and she asked all the questions I didn't think to ask and didn't know to ask. She's a nurse so that helps. She stayed with me, listened to me cry and told me how strong I was. She helped me tell my parents, because talking was difficult and processing was difficult. They had too many questions and I just couldn't give any answers they needed. Sarah was amazing and my friend Stacy who went to my house and brought me things and got the girls where they needed to be. Sarah took Kayla and then arranged for Michael to have Riley. In this moment where I was unable to care for myself, my friends stepped up and in and cared for the girls and I. The next few days were difficult to say the least. Occupational and physical therapy every day and more tests like MRA's and MRI's. I was exhausted and drained. I felt so tired all the time. I had a slight droop on my mouth and a foot drop, that just means that my foot dragged when I walked. I couldn't bathe myself, I had difficulty talking and processing my thoughts and weakness in my arm. My stroke was in the cerebellum, the part of the brain that controls balance. I had to depend on others to care for my basic needs and that was hard for me. I was happily independent and proud to be that way, so this was a strange and unwelcome change. Then in all my confusion, fear and uncertainty, in walks the parental units. The monster looks at me and says you look fine, let's find a doctor and see what the truth is. BITCH! Like I woke up and said, "how can I get my parents to come see me? Hmm... I think I will fake a stroke and get MRI results to prove it." What a moron she is. She claims she spent 45 minutes discussing my health with my doctor, which by the way, I gave no permission for; hello HIPAA violation!

The doctor shut her lying theory down with facts and truth. I had in fact had a stroke and I had deficits and they wanted me to go to a rehab center until I recovered. Well, once they said that little piece of nonsense, I was like absolutely not. I can do everything at home. Reluctantly, they agreed and let me go home. They set me up with occupational therapy and physical therapy at home. I had to relearn balance and coordination. The simple things that I took for granted, were sometimes impossible now. My girls were waiting on me and I had friends bringing us food and groceries. My boss sent dinners and flowers.

Therapy sucked, bad. I hated every second of it, but I had to do it. I had to install a shower bar and that was the most defeating and disappointing part of it all. I now needed a bar to get me in and out of the shower and I was 32 years old! I wanted no one to see me that way. I didn't care to date, go anywhere or be around people. I stayed home or went to work. I was so fearful I would have another stroke and I was afraid people would know I had one just by walking around. I didn't want pity or the looks, I wanted to be treated just as I was before. My professors were kind and patient. I worked, took care of the girls and went to school. I wanted normalcy and I didn't want to live in fear. I quit smoking, gave up soda and started little by little changing how I ate. I took my meds and did what I was supposed to do. But a month later, another setback. I was doing homework, Kayla was in her room and Riley was watching a movie in my room. I needed quiet and the girls understood when I was doing school work that I needed minimal interruptions. I was typing a paper and got dizzy and felt weird almost instantly. I texted Kayla and she came running out and called Sarah, she told her to call 911 and stay calm. Kayla dialed and I listened to her voice shake and she paced back and forth continuing to check on me and her sister simultaneously and remaining calm. Riley had no clue what was going on; she was so into her movie.

Rescue got to me rather quickly and immediately looked me over and then carried me out of the house. Kayla held on to Riley who was now in Kayla's arms crying. Sarah ran in while they were loading me up and stayed with the girls and then followed me in the ambulance. Going to an ER code stroke is quite scary. You are wheeled into a trauma room, followed by so many people undressing you and taking vitals and yelling things out. It was as if I was watching everything happen to someone else. I couldn't speak and that was freaking me out. My brain and mouth weren't connecting, but I knew what I wanted to say. They rushed me to a CT where a neurologist was waiting and came in, looked me in the eye and said, "I've got you, don't worry". They told me I had a TIA this time and a night in the neuro ICU was in store for me since I was unable to speak still. Sarah had to leave, and she went to my house and got Kayla and took Riley to Michael. When I got released, I had to see my neurologist who told me that since I had another stroke within a month of the first one my recurrent risk was now more elevated; great, just what I needed. Anyhow, I went home and committed to changing everything in my life that was toxic or harmful. I prayed a little here and there and began to try healthy cooking. It wasn't until a few years later in 2015 when I started working at a Health and Wellness company that I realized how truly unhealthy I was and what a disservice I was doing to myself. I am committed to exercising daily and eating right every meal. I started seeing my friend Jamie's social media posts about the 21 Day Fix through Beachbody and I reached out to her to see what it was all about. Shortly after that call, I ordered the 21 Day Fix Extreme, because I can never be ordinary, and I anxiously waited for it's arrival. The day it came, I opened it with as much excitement as Ralphie opening his Red Rider BeeBee Gun. This was it, this was what was going to make me healthy. I worked out with Autumn 7 days a week and ate well and began to feel strong and was seeing changes in my body and a confidence that left shortly after I met Terrell. When I was in high school, I was thin and fit and active so this later in life sedentary lifestyle was uncomfortable, but comfortable at the same time.

I realized that Riley was looking to me for inspiration and guidance. I realized that while I had been doing a terrible disservice to myself, I also was doing one to her and Kayla. They needed a healthy mom to care for them and navigate them through their lives, and I was not that. After the first stroke, I committed to not only be healthy, but to be a better mom and person. It wasn't like I was this horrible monstrosity that the monster had others believe, I was just flawed, angry and full of pain. For many years, it was just me and my girls and extended family. I had essentially been on my own since that day the monster and I came to blows and I ran out of that horrible home and into my future. I made many mistakes and many things I would have done differently, but they all made me who I am now. It took me so long to believe I was lovable and deserved to be loved. It took finding my way into therapy and finding my way to God to begin to heal and believe. Pain is the body's way of knowing we are healing and I found comfort in that. I found solace in my thoughts, my pain and my children. My life was and is still not what I envisioned from my bedroom as a teenager. I would sit in that room, mostly because I was always grounded, but I would dream. I would imagine my future as a doctor and could hear them paging me. I could see the big home, happy family and 3 children. I could see what my whole future was and would be. I could only imagine greatness for myself, because that was what my mom had always told me. She told me I was supposed to be great. I was supposed to be a doctor and go to University of Miami and live in Coral Gables in some obscene home with mature trees. UM was always my dream, until I got pregnant, then all the dreams took a back seat to motherhood. So, instead of being a full time student, I became a full time fan; an acceptable trade off, without the student loan debt.

Chapter Twenty-Two

The Break in My Reality

$2$014 was a difficult year for my girls and I. That was the

same year that Michael ran off to Florida and Riley went into therapy. It was a trying time for her and she and I were trying to navigate her new normal all while Kayla was dealing with her Crohn's Diagnosis and how she was feeling. The year before Kayla was diagnosed and it was very difficult for us all. We had to learn what made her feel awful and she endured constant trips to the doctor and hospital. My Aunt Mindy and I were at odds and hadn't spoken in months. Her and my Uncle did not believe that Kayla had Crohn's let alone understand that she had to get treatment for it. Kayla and I were left to deal with her new illness all the while, taking Riley back and forth to therapy to understand her anger towards her dad leaving her. I felt like nothing could go right and nothing would be good for my girls anymore, they were both hurting in different ways. Watching Kayla endure Crohn's and be as sick as she was on a daily basis was difficult to say the least. I watched my beautiful, strong, funny child become a fighter and fraile all at the same time. During this struggle, Kayla felt that it was best for her to live in Tennessee with Mindy and Joe and I agreed.

She was angry at life for her circumstances and I blamed myself for her newest ailment. The combination of how we both felt got us nowhere in our relationship. I knew that if we were ever going to be the mother daughter I had always dreamt we would be, I had to let her go and not fight it. It broke me. My little girl had left and needed to be away from me to be happy. That pill was one that I choked on daily. I prayed that God would guide her and protect her and one day bring her back to me. I wrote to her, letters that would never leave my mind or my journal. I told her of all that was going on in Riley and I's life and how much we missed her and how I needed my girl back.

A few years later, my whole world changed, and Kayla came back to me. We worked HARD on repairing our relationship and owning up to what we had done and said to hurt each other. Through the hurt, we began to heal and become stronger than ever. She is who I go to when I need a harsh truth or just a funny conversation. She has become my friend and my daughter. Tennessee was where she belonged and that is what made her the woman she is now. She found her soulmate there and in him she got a family that showered her with kindness and love daily. Kayla got married on Labor Day 2020 and a few months later found out she had become pregnant.

Kayla planned and executed a beautiful wedding that was full of laughter, love and the blending of two families; and my baby changing her name. Now she was a woman, and I was in awe of her. I sat on the swings outside the barn she got married at with my Brandon and thanked God that he had let me be there for that moment in her life and that she wanted me there. Brandon wrapped me up in his arms and I felt more loved in that moment than I had in my entire life. We sent the bride and groom off to their honeymoon and to begin their new life and I headed back to North Carolina.

It was on Halloween 2020, I received a call that would forever change my life. It was 8:30pm and Kayla FaceTimed me, no different than any of our other calls, since that is how we communicate. I love it, because I get to look at her beautiful face. Kayla said, "Mom, I have to tell you something." My heart sank and I had no idea what it could be. This kid has always had a flair for the shock factor and for all I knew she was moving to Costa Rica or something. I took a deep breath and said, "Ok baby what is it?" Her husband, Austin, came into the screen and they both exclaimed, "We are pregnant!" I began to cry and could not believe my ears. My baby girl was going to be a mommy. Funny enough a week before, I told her on FaceTime that she looked different in the face and that I thought she was pregnant, she laughed it off and we didn't speak of it again. But this moment had come, the second biggest moment in her life. The stick turned and many others as well and it was real. I looked at her through my tear filled eyes and told her I loved her and that it was a girl. She didn't believe me. I asked when this baby was due, "July 16th" she told me. I said, "She will be here on July 4th weekend." Kayla laughed it off.

But a few weeks later, through her terrible morning sickness, she had hyperemesis gravida, AKA the Kate Middleton disease, it was time to do her gender reveal. Austin's parents and I sat on pins and needles on FaceTime, they thought this baby was a boy and I thought girl and Kayla had come to my side on the gender as well. Poppers in hand, Kayla and Austin pulled and pink shot out! I was so excited and Austin's mom couldn't believe it. We had a baby girl to get ready for. Kayla and Austin picked out a name, one that we all loved and adored. Austin's mom embroidered bibs, outfits and bought more bows for her hair than I knew existed. We took care of what these two new parents needed. We made sure that they had what they needed to feel like they could be successful parents and money was no object for my baby girl. Kayla told me on Halloween what she wanted the baby to call me, and it overwhelmed me and excited me all at the same time. She told me that I was not like normal grandmas, so I deserved a different name. Her and Austin smiled at each other and told me my name, 'Lovie' it was perfect. I was humbled and honored to be this baby's Lovie.

Memorial Day weekend we celebrated the baby's arrival with a Lil Cutie themed baby shower. The day was about Kayla and Austin and no one else mattered. They were showered with love, gifts and food; all of Kayla's favorites. Kayla didn't have the easiest pregnancy, at all and I worried about her all the time and being four hours away from her. I became a Labor Doula so I could be in the delivery room, it was our way around COVID restrictions. Austin embraced learning how to help Kayla in her delivery while I taught them both what I had learned in Doula class. Austin was amazing and supportive with Kayla. I could not have asked for a more perfect person to be my daughter's soul mate. He gets her, he respects her and most of all he doesn't try and change her; instead he encourages her and defends her fiercely.

Kayla went to the doctor on Tuesday, June 29th and they scheduled her induction for July 14th, she went home and continued her nightly walks and was focused on delivery; she was done being pregnant. Every mom gets there, that point where it is eviction time and the exhaustion of being pregnant has become too much to bear. Austin's mom and I had been saying that we felt the baby would be here on July

2nd for months. For some reason we both felt that particular day, we were in sync with it and my bags had been packed for weeks ready to go when the baby was. July 1st, Kayla decided she was going to make the Midwives Brew, a drink known to induce labor naturally. She called me on FaceTime as she was beginning to drink it.

Austin and I cheered her on and encouraged her to get it down. It was a struggle for her because the taste was awful. She hung up with me when she finished, feeling the need to use the restroom and my phone rang 20 minutes later with her telling me she had projectile vomited the brew all over the bathroom. I worried that she had drunk this whole thing and it would not work for her, because she had her heart set on it working. We spoke for a few minutes and I went off to sleep. July 2nd, at 1am, my phone rings; "Mom, my water broke, get in the car!" I jumped up and got coffee in me, and tried my best to wake up, since I had taken a muscle relaxer.. I went in to get Riley up and she was already awake, sitting on her bed, looking at pictures of her and her sister. I told her, "Sissy's water broke, we have to go now!" She was so excited and helped gather our things and I got dressed and brushed my teeth and Kayla called back and asked if we were on the road, I told her we were just about to leave. I was incredibly nervous to make that drive at night through the mountains, alone, but she needed me and I wasn't missing this for anything.

At 2am, Riley and I got in the car, took a moment to gather ourselves and prayed together. We prayed we would make it there safely and that Kayla would have a smooth delivery and I would make it be there for her. Off into the night we went, and the rain began shortly after we entered the interstate. It was pitch black, raining and I was determined to get us there. Riley was amazing and stayed up almost the entire time to keep me awake. She fell asleep for a little bit and in that moment I hydroplaned and just took a breath and we were good. I thanked God for being with us and continued on. Kayla called to give me updates through the drive, she was only 2-3 centimeters dilated so I had time.

We made it into Knoxville, and were about 12 minutes from the hospital when on the radio came Kenny Chesney's song, 'There Goes My Life'. This song had so much value to me, and to Kayla, it had always been my song for her. It is a song about becoming a parent as a teen and how these two teen parents navigated it and then watched their little girl go to college; but from the fathers perspective. It still takes my breath away when I hear it and I think about Kayla as a baby, with her curly hair and bright eyes full of hope and love. I began to cry singing this song and thought that this was God telling me that I would make it there in time and reminding me how far Kayla and I have come in 24 years. I pulled up to the hospital, nervous and excited all at the same time. I settled Riley in the car with snacks and the keys because of COVID she was not allowed in the hospital and kissed Riley and ran inside to get to my girl.

Chapter Twenty-Three

Becoming Lovie

*A*t 6:30am, I walked in the hospital room, and my baby girl

was lying in the bed in pain and a little high from the stadol that they had given her. Austin and his mom were in there, he was sleeping, and his mom updated me on what was going on with Kayla. Kayla was watching The Fresh Prince of Bel Air on the TV and I reminded her of the story of her birth. I too got stadol and it made me think my friend was Jefferey the Butler from The Fresh Prince of Bel Air, it was so symbolic for me.

Kayla was clear and concise on what she wanted during delivery and left room in her birth plan for the unknown and unforeseen; I was so proud of her and all the research she had done. She was prepared to be a mommy and prepared for what to expect in delivery. I continued to check on Riley in the car, there were no waiting room options due to COVID restrictions, and then Austin's dad snagged up Riley and they hung out together while we all were in the hospital with Kayla. The pain had begun to be a struggle for Kayla even though she had been given the stadol to help, it proved to not be enough. Kayla wanted to get up and pee, and while standing, swaying in Austin's arms, she demanded an epidural. We all looked at each other, because she didn't want one, and was clear on that. She demanded it again, and then we knew she was serious about wanting it. We got the nurse and shortly after the anesthesiologist came in and it was epidural time.

The nurse checked her again for dilation before the epidural and she was at 5 centimeters dilated, we still had a ways to go and the epidural could slow everything down. Austin's mom and I hung out in the hallway while Kayla and Austin got set up for the epidural. She thought the baby would be here by 4pm, I thought later in the day since she was getting the epidural. I listened to my baby girl moan in pain and it was overwhelming to hear. Austin's mom and I looked at each other and smiled and said, "July 2nd!" We were right, this little lady was coming on the day we had predicted all along. We went back in the room and all tended to a different part of Kayla, the moms were at her hands and Austin rubbed her feet while she moaned and riled in pain. Austin and I swapped and he held her hand through it and I rubbed her feet. In the epidural's presence, the baby was difficult to find on the monitor, so the nurse inserted an internal monitor on the baby's head so she could monitor the baby's heartbeat. While she did that she was able to tell us that in the 20 minutes since the epidural had been placed, Kayla was at 8 centimeters dilated.

A few minutes later, Kayla said her butt hurt and she felt like she needed to push. The nurse checked her and she was 10 centimeters! It was 30 minutes after the epidural, it happened so fast. The staff came in and turned the room over quickly for delivery and the nurse began to tell us all where we were to be and what to do. Austin and his mom held Kayla's legs and I tended to her hands and kept her calm. I watched while my brave, strong daughter pushed her daughter into the birth canal like she had done this before. No words, no noise, just focused pushing; she did amazing. We watched as the baby girl's head began to peek out, and the nurse played with her hair, she had tons of hair; just like her mommy did.

The baby crowned, and the doctor barely made it in and into her sterile wear before Kayla and the baby were ready to push more. Another set of pushes and we had a head and then shoulders and then, a beautiful baby girl. We all cried as she popped into the world, and stared at her in complete and total awe and love. Austin cut the cord and they reveled in the beautiful little lady that they had created. Austin and his mom followed the baby with the nurse to check her out in the room and I stayed with my baby. I leaned in and kissed her on her forehead, we cried together, it was a brief moment for just us and I loved it. Moments later, with her APGAR done, she was cleaned up a bit; then back to her mommy's arms, her little bundle of love. The nurse handed this beautiful creation back to her momma and instantly, I was taken back to the day Kayla was born. I watched my baby girl calm her baby girl and in that moment, we had come full circle. This teenage mother that everyone said would neer amount to anything, just assisted her daughter in labor and was now a grandma. I took a breath, internally thanked God for a safe delivery and healthy baby and kissed my baby and hers.

Welcome to the world our delicate, River Blue.

I asked the nurse what time she arrived, we were all so focused on helping Kayla that no one looked at a clock. She looked at me and said, "10:31am". Kayla was over the moon, and exclaimed, "I got my

Halloween baby after all!" Kayla LOVES Halloween, she would make it a national holiday if she had it her way and it would be more than a day. Weighing in at 6 pounds even and 19 inches long, our delicate baby, River Blue, was brought into the world surrounded by love, many tears, nursing staff, nursing students and happiness. At that moment, I was given something I never thought I would see, a granddaughter. When I had that stroke, and the many after, I never thought I would live long enough to see this and now I had and it was breathtaking to me. Austin held his daughter and looked at me and said, "Lovie you wanna hold her?" Lovie. WOW. I'm Lovie! Lovie absolutely wanted to hold her and I looked into her eyes and she held my finger and I was instantly in love with this little lady. She was perfection personified and had a full head of hair with the most beautiful eyes that almost looked like they could see inside of you. She was alert and stared at everyone that held her, it was like that part in Breaking Dawn Part Two, when Reneesmee would show everyone her first memory of them. She looked at me that way, like she knew me, while I talked to her and cried. I had made it to see her come into the world and be there for her mommy; all was right in my world.

But, we had the extended family's feelings and disgust to deal with. Mindy hated that I was in the room and she was not, which, why would she be? She has this unnatural, unfounded claim on Kayla and thinks as if I am worthless to Kayla. So, naturally, her daughter would feel the same. But, Kayla's godfather, Mindy's son Jared, did not feel like them. He called to congratulate me and we both talked about how we couldn't believe Kayla was a mom now! I sent him pictures I had taken and we ended our call and he called Kayla. But he had called me to talk to me, that meant so much to me. He was the only member of the extended family to do that. Not even Samantha called me, my so-called best friend.

Samantha and I had a falling out the year before because I didn't think her new boyfriend was worthy of her and he gave me massive abuser vibes, with stories she had been telling me. Something about him was not right to me, and I didn't care to learn anything at all about him. I thought our relationship of a lifetime was strong enough to endure my opinion of her new man, but I was wrong. He then began to message me and FaceBook call me incessantly one day and I ignored him and it angered him. The next day, Samantha and I had it out about him on the phone because I did respond to him and told him how I felt. She listened to me and told me that he and I were the two most important people in her life and she needed us to get along. I told her I would be cordial, but I didn't like him and thought he would hurt her physically and told her to tell him to never contact me again. She agreed and we ended the call on decent terms. A few days later, I woke up to a 12:30am long message from this guy, telling me that he was going nowhere and Samantha and him would be together and there was nothing I could do about it; I just had to deal with it. I texted Samantha and asked her to please have him stop messaging me and she defended him.

It was right then, within that moment, she said the thing that would always be associated with her and how she truly feels about me. She told me that, "No one in my family liked or loved me, they tolerated me because of her and I was bitter and vicious." Those words were meant to hurt and that they did just that. She called me a couple months later, in an "attempt" to make things right but refused to apologize for what she said and instead laughed and said, "you will always be bitter and single and you are just jealous of me and Bob!" She then hung up and I texted her and told her how sad this all was that she chose him over me and would not even apologize for her words. If she had done that, maybe we could have moved forward, but not even taking responsibility for the hurt you cause, is no one I want in my life. I own up to my mistakes and the hurt I have caused. I again, reached out to her after Kayla's bridal shower and said we should put this all behind us, that if she didn't want to apologize, I forgive her regardless and nothing until the day before Kayla's wedding.

She sends me a generic text saying, "can't believe Kayla's getting married tomorrow". I responded briefly stating, I couldn't believe it either and then got in the car to drive to Kayla. During my drive, I get the most ridiculous text from her mom telling me how awful of a person I was for not giving Samantha a proper response. Seriously! I was about to get in the car and drive for 4 hours, I responded, it wasn't to your liking, that is your issue not mine. We briefly spoke at Kayla's wedding, but her and I will never be the same ever again. The moment she chose a man she had been dating a few months and seen only once in person over me, I was no longer her best friend.

So, Kayla received calls from Mindy, incessantly. Mindy told her that when I was gone, she would come and see the baby. Really! You can't put aside your unfounded disdain for me to come and see this new baby? I didn't understand it and I kept my opinion to myself until

Kayla asked me. I had told Kayla that she would feel different towards that side of the family once the baby was here and Austin would too. I told her that her little family she created was all that mattered, the rest of us should conform or exit. I have never been good enough in my family's eyes, be it my father or Mindy, it doesn't matter they all see me as not good enough. But, what I have learned through prayer, therapy, time, and people's actions is that I am worthy and I am good enough. I remind myself regularly that God made me perfectly and wonderfully just how I am; no one's opinion of me matters except his.

So, Sandy, Dad, Samantha, Mindy, Joe and Jamie, your judgment of me is unfounded, unwelcome and frankly unrealistic, I'll send you a mirror so you can see where you can shove your questions about my worthiness to be in my own daughters life and granddaughters. That and the shame in your own selves, are right where it belongs; in your reflection; not towards me. Let me also be perfectly clear here. I have not "lost" great people in my life. People have been exiled from my life due to how they have treated me, those same people are not good or even great. So, at the end of the day, I chose my own peace and happiness over any "family" member's approval. The only approval I need is God's and my children, otherwise, no one else matters enough for me to care.

I don't know what will come of my future, my relationships, my life, my children and grandchildren anything, but I do know that the same girl that was crying and cutting herself in middle school to not feel has begun the long hard process of healing and has a bright future if she is not afraid to explore and uncover the shame she has carried her entire life. This woman is now armed with the confidence she gained in kickboxing, the love of friends that truly accept me and children that love me; and a beautiful and new granddaughter that lights up my life. I never thought I would be able to see the day that my Kayla would become a mommy or even get married and I have seen both. I pray that God allows me the grace to see what future Riley has in store and that I get to be a part of it. Riley is my sidekick, she is the Rory Gilmore to my Lorelai Gilmore and she and I have a bond that cannot be broken or dismantled.

Watch out world, I have my sassy pants on and they are making my ass look fantastic!

Milton Keynes UK
Ingram Content Group UK Ltd.
UKHW040020010324
438686UK00004B/73